Beatitudes:
Success 101

DAVE WILLIAMS

Beatitudes: Success 101

*Principles Of Success From
The Lips Of Jesus*

DAVE WILLIAMS

Beatitudes: Success 101
Principles Of Success From The Lips Of Jesus

Unless otherwise noted, Scripture quotations are taken from the King James Version of the Bible.

Scripture quotations noted TLB are from *The Living Bible*, Copyright ©1971. Used by permission of Tyndale House Publishers, Inc., Wheaton, Illinois 60189. All rights reserved.

Scripture quotations marked NLT are from *The Holy Bible, New Living Translation*, Copyright ©1996. Used by permission of Tyndale House Publishers, Inc., Wheaton, Illinois 60189. All rights reserved.

Copyright ©2003 by David R. Williams

ISBN   0-938020-68-4

First Printing 2003

Cover Design: Joe Oberlin & Gerard R. Jones

Published by

DECAPOLIS
PUBLISHING

BOOKS BY DAVE WILLIAMS

15 Big Causes of Failure
36 Minutes with the Pastor
7 Sign Posts on the Road to Spiritual Maturity
ABCs of Success and Happiness
Angels: They Are Watching You!
Art of Pacesetting Leadership
Beatitudes: Success 101
Cave of Depression
Christian Job Hunters Handbook
Deception, Delusion, & Destruction
Developing the Spirit of a Conqueror
End Times Bible Prophecy
Faith Goals
Filled: With The Mightiest Power in the Universe
Genuine Prosperity
Getting to Know Your Heavenly Father
Gifts That Shape Your Life & Change Your World
Grand Finale
Grief and Mourning
Growing Up in Our Father's Family
Heard from the Lord Lately?
How to be High Performance Believer
Lonely in the Midst of a Crowd
Miracle Results of Fasting
New Life...The Start of Something Wonderful
New Life-Spanish
Patient Determination
Questions I Have Answered
Radical Fasting
Radical Healing
Radical Forgiveness
Regaining Your Spiritual Momentum

MORE BOOKS BY DAVE WILLIAMS

Revival Power of Music
Road to Radical Riches
Secret of Power with God
Slain in the Spirit
Somebody Out There Needs You
Supernatural Gifts of the Holy Spirit
Supernatural Soul Winning
The AIDS Plague
The Beauty of Holiness
The Desires of your Heart
The Jezebel Spirit
The Pastor's Minute
The Pastor's Pay
The Presence Of God
The World Beyond
Tongues & Interpretation
Understanding Spiritual Gifts
What To Do If You Miss the Rapture
Your Pastor: The Key To Your Personal Wealth.

Contents

The true measure of how you perform will come in the course of life, and you will have to grade yourself.

Introduction

It was a warm day, with winds blowing in from the lake causing the flowers on the hillside to sway gently. The fishing boats were visible on the water, moving silently amidst glimmers of sunlight. The people could see the town from the hillside — there the synagogue; over there the marketplace where vendors were putting out their fruits and vegetables; there a few houses by the shore.

The crowd murmured and laughed as they followed Jesus. He led them up a hillside and brought them to a place on the hill where the land curved below Him, creating a natural amphitheater. He sat down and waited for everyone of His disciples to gather in closer and sit down to listen.

I can imagine Peter thinking, "I'm so glad to be out here in the sunshine. I'd hate to be one of those students of the law, shut up indoors all day."

What he and the disciples didn't know, as they took their seats on the ground, was that class was just about to begin. Jesus was starting a new semester, and this was the first lecture. Some would later call it the Beatitudes, or the Sermon on the Mount, but it could just as easily have been called Success 101.

That day Jesus gave the disciples the underlying principles for successful living. It was the first thing He taught them after telling them to "Follow me." He summed up how the Kingdom worked, and how the disciples could make it work for them. He put success in their hands.

Thank God that we have the lecture notes from that class period! More than that, we have the exact transcript, as if we were there ourselves, sitting at Jesus' feet and drinking in His words. Together, we can be students of Success 101.

The point of the class was to teach them how to be happy and prosperous by:

- Being teachable, trusting, and humble.

- Mourning properly.

- Being nonjudgmental.

- Being gentle and gracious.

- Having a spiritual appetite.

- Being merciful.

- Being pure in heart.

- Being a peacemaker.

- Being persecuted.

All of us need to fit this description more each day. Maybe on some of them you would give yourself high marks, but on others you struggle. If so, it's time to go back to school!

This course has no written exam (but there is a pretty serious final!). There are no pop quizzes or midterms, number two pencils, or blue books. The true measure of how you perform will come in the course of your life, and you will have to grade yourself.

Are you a successful person?

Are you growing more merciful?

Less judgmental?

More teachable, gentle and hungry for God's Kingdom?

Do you mourn properly?

Do you make peace?

Is your heart kept pure?

You may wonder why Jesus chose to teach people outdoors, on hillsides and from fishing boats rather than inside a classroom. It's because He knew that was where His teaching would be carried out. What good was the knowledge He gave them if it wasn't immediately put into practice? So He placed His lectern in the marketplace and taught where it mattered.

That's our lesson too: put these things into practice. Then, when the final test comes and God judges us according to what we have done, you can look back and be thankful you took His course in success. Who knows? You may get an A+!

Chapter One

Blessed Are
The Teachable And Trusting

Dad turned the last screw, and the training wheels fell off of the bike. Joey took a deep breath. He'd never ridden without them before, but he could tell by the look on his father's face that it would be all right.

"Get on," his dad said, "I'll push."

Joey mounted the bike and gripped the handle-bars in determination, then put his feet on the pedals as his dad held the bike steady. He could see the training wheels laying on the driveway.

"Look straight ahead," Dad whispered into Joey's ear. "Hold the handlebars tight, but not too tight, and keep pedaling. The slower you go, the harder it is to stay up. I'll give you a push."

The bike moved forward, and Joey could feel that the training wheels were no longer there to keep him from tipping over. He gained speed as Dad pushed faster, and then with one final shove Joey was on his own.

Oh, the joy he felt gliding across the dirt field! The front tire wobbled, but he kept it steady, pedaling for all he was worth. He was exhilarated and scared as he came closer to the neighbor's lawn, full of thick grass, suddenly realizing he had to change directions or crash into their cement bird bath, and beyond that the clothes line.

Joey yanked the wheel to one side, forgetting that the training wheels weren't there to keep him upright, and in a tangle of handlebars and limbs went tumbling onto the lawn. He opened his eyes to see the blue sky above and his dad running, smiling from across the field.

"Good job, Joey!" he said. "I knew you could do it!"

He hadn't hit the bird bath or the clothes line, and grass had cushioned the fall, but he did hit his shin on the pedal and it throbbed. Dad picked him up.

"That was terrific. A lot better than I did my first time. Ready to go again?"

Joey wasn't sure, but he agreed and by the end of the day had learned to brake and put his foot down without falling over. Within a week he rode around the neighborhood like an old pro.

Some people grow up and lose their ability to learn, to be taught, to trust. And yet Jesus called those things keys to happiness.

> Blessed *are* the poor in spirit: for theirs is the kingdom of heaven.
>
> —Matthew 5:3

Before we see what it means to be poor in spirit, we need to ask what Jesus meant by this word "blessed." It can sound so churchy, spiritual and stuffy, but the word is actually very straightforward. It means:

• To be happy and overflowing with indescribable joy.

• To have special gifts, advantages, and benefits conferred upon you by God Himself.

• To receive a personal expression of congratulations.

People have strange ideas of what brings happiness. A greeting card I saw once said, "Happiness means never having to say you're sorry." Not only is that inaccurate — all of us have to say we're sorry sometimes, even to those closest to us — but it falls well-short of what Jesus meant by "blessed."

I once heard on the radio that if men want to be happy they should never marry a pretty woman. A pretty woman, the commentator said, makes a man look small and ugly, so a man should get an ugly wife to make him look better!

I'm not sure ugliness is the path to happiness any more than beauty is. Perhaps a better way is to have joy bubbling up inside of you. One time a lady was visiting a church that was steeped in tradition. It had ivy growing up the brick walls, and everyone filed in silently for Sunday service. This Sunday, in particular, a powerful evangelist was invited to speak there, and after the stodgy singing and announcements were finished he got up and preached with fire and passion. The lady visitor could barely help herself when he said something that excited her, and she hopped up and said, "Praise the Lord!!" The whole church turned around and looked at her. An usher walked over and said, "I know you're visiting, but we don't do that in this church. Please, be a little more reserved."

A few minutes later the evangelist hit another high point and she jumped up and said, "Hallelujah!" At that point, two ushers walked over, picked her up out of the pew and started carrying her out of the church. She looked at the preacher and said, "Look at me! When Jesus rode into Jerusalem, He was on *one* donkey, but it takes *two* to carry me!"

That woman had outrageous joy that she could barely contain. Perhaps it overflowed a little too much for that church, but I imagine there were others there that day who wished they had even a fraction of what she had!

There's a glow about people who are blessed. They have special benefits and advantages from God. They have learned the secrets to successful living.

How do we get that kind of happiness?

A State Of Humility

The first lesson Jesus taught that day was, "Blessed are the poor in spirit." Did He mean blessed are the poor in their bank accounts? Blessed are those who have empty pockets? Empty billfolds? Who are in severe debt?

Jesus wasn't talking about financial poverty. He wasn't talking about money at all. I was taught for much of my life that poor people are more blessed than rich people, but after reading the Bible more closely, I realized that wasn't true. Jesus didn't say blessed are the financially poor but the poor *in spirit*. He was talking about a state of humility, where we're willing to be guided and taught from outside our-selves. Being poor in spirit has three components:

- To be teachable

- To admit personal inadequacy

- To trust God to supply whatever you lack

You and I both know people who are know-it-alls. You can't tell them anything they don't already know. They know more theology than the pastor, more about children than the nursery workers, more about music than the choir director, and more about evangelism than the outreach pastor. They don't need a Bible training course. They could have *written* the Bible.

That's being unteachable, and it repels happiness.

Being teachable means being able to admit our personal inadequacy. The truth is, not one of us has anything to offer God. We are hopeless unless His grace empowers us. Yes, the Bible commands us to confess that we are mighty in Christ, but only after we first confess our own personal inability to accomplish anything without God.

> ...for without me ye can do nothing.
>
> —John 15:5c
>
> ...with God all things are possible.
>
> —Matthew 19:26c

One of my favorite verses is Psalms 127:1a.

Except the LORD build the house, they labour in vain that build it:

—**Psalms 127:1**

If the Lord doesn't do the building in your life, home, church, ministry or business then you're beating your head against the wall. The way to be blessed is to acknowledge that truth right up-front. That's why Jesus gave this lesson before any other.

Humble In Frame

Orel Hershiser was a famous pitcher for the Los Angeles Dodgers and was a World Series MVP. He wrote a book that included a chapter called "Johnny and the Hymn Singer," which related his experience on Johnny Carson's Tonight Show. Out of the blue, Johnny asked him, "Do you ever sing when you're out there on the mound?" Orel tried to brush the question off, but Johnny wasn't going to let him. Finally Orel said, "Yes, I sing to myself." Johnny pushed a little farther and said, "We'd like to hear you sing." The audience cheered him on and he agreed. He said, "This song sums it all up. 'Praise God from whom all blessings flow. Praise Him all creatures here below. Praise Him above ye heavenly hosts. Praise Father, Son and Holy Ghost. Amen.'"

The place became silent and Johnny must have thought, "What did I get myself into?" Orel said, "I

21

have been honored for being a baseball star, but I realize how inadequate I am without God. When I'm on the mound, I ask God to be my adequacy."

Why did God honor Orel Hershiser, lifting him up to a place as a role model and hero who played in the World Series and was on the Tonight Show? Because he was poor in spirit.

Samuel Morse invented Morse Code and the telegraph, the first long-distance communication system. It is still used today by pilots to identify navigational radio beams.

A friend asked Morse one time, "Did you ever come to a standstill in your experiments while inventing the telegraph?" He said, "Many times. When I did, I got on my knees and prayed, 'Lord, if you see fit to use me in making this device that will benefit mankind, I pray that you would give me more light on the subject.'" Soon an idea would come to him, and he would get closer to the final product. That was his method of invention.

The first words that went across the telegraph system were, "What God hath wrought?" Morse said that though people bestowed honors on him, he never felt like he deserved them. He believed he was a channel that God seemed pleased to use.

Samuel Morse was poor in spirit too.

Those are the kinds of people God will use, honor, and empower to bring miracles into other people's lives.

Access To Heaven

Jesus said of the poor in spirit, "For theirs is the Kingdom of Heaven." Did that mean they would have special entry into the pearly gates come Judgment Day? A bigger mansion in a more elite neighborhood in Heaven? No, Jesus was talking about the Kingdom here and now. He said the Kingdom of God is within you. The poor in spirit have access to the Kingdom that the haughty in spirit don't.

Why? Because they readily admit they don't have the power to solve the challenges they face, and when they ask for it, God sends power and angels and provision from Heaven to fill the need. It is only the poor in spirit who can say, "I can do everything through Him who gives me strength" (Philippians 4:13).

Many people fail this first lesson of Success 101. They retain their pride, their self-sufficiency; they're full of themselves.

> Pride *goeth* before destruction, and an haughty spirit before a fall.
>
> —Proverbs 16:18

Famous American Ben Franklin didn't quite grasp the importance of spiritual poverty. One time he made up a list of twelve virtues he thought were the most important. He planned to work on one a week for twelve weeks until he reached his idea of perfection. He came up with temperance, silence, order, resolve, prudence, industry, sincerity, justice, moderation, cleanliness, tranquility and chastity. He showed the list to a friend who pointed out to Ben that he had left one off — humility. Ben replied, "Oh yes, I'll put it at the bottom of the list."

Franklin and many others put it at the bottom of the list, but Jesus puts it at the top of the list, and the top of His lesson on success. He said whoever humbles himself before God shall be lifted up. This is what poverty in spirit is all about. It's a key that opens the door to blessedness, advantage, benefit, getting the most out of life, and having access to the Kingdom of Heaven.

Someone said it's easier to irrigate low land than high ground. Likewise, it's easier to bring fruit forth from a soul that is teachable, trusting and humble. The publican in Jesus' story said "I sure am glad I'm not like that sinner over there. I tithe, and I fast twice a week, and I go to the synagogue every time the doors are open." Next to him was a poor bum who fell on his face, beat his chest and said, "God, be merciful to me, a sinner." Jesus said the poor bum was justified before God; not the publican confessing his own righteousness. One was poor in spirit, the other full of his own spiritual "wealth."

F. B. Meyer wrote, "I used to think that God's gifts were on shelves one above the other, and the taller you grow in Christian character, the easier it is to reach those gifts. Now I find that all of God's greatest gifts are on the lower shelves, so we always have to stoop down to get them."

That is the posture you and I should have as we seek to be blessed.

Next we'll look at a promise that seems to run exactly opposite to what being blessed is all about.

Different people have different ideas about how to mourn and for how long. But how can a person who's in mourning be blessed?

Chapter Two

Blessed Are
Those Who Mourn

Have you ever seen someone who just lost a loved one? Their eyes are sunken in from sadness and bloodshot from crying. Their skin looks pale, their steps are tentative. They typically dress in black for a while and go into a time of mourning that can take months to complete.

They attend the funeral and are forced to be seen at their greatest point of grief. They suddenly are met with the most unwelcome of obligations: choosing a plot and a casket, going through the deceased person's finances and possessions, and making sure the right taxes are paid and the will is executed properly.

Usually you look at such a person and think, "I'm glad I'm not in that position."

And yet the second lesson Jesus gave is that those people are blessed.

> **Blessed are those who mourn, for they will be comforted.**
>
> —Matthew 5:4

How in the world can this be true? How can someone be happy in mourning? Is this God's way of telling us to buck up, move on, not take things so hard? Or does it mean something deeper?

I was listening to people in my church having a conversation one day, and they asked me, "Pastor Dave, how long do you think a person should wait after their spouse dies before they start courting another person?" Before I could answer, one of the women who looked upset pointed to her husband and said, "Ask him how long he'd wait." I did and he said, "I'd give her three days before I started looking for another wife." She looked at him in renewed shock and said, "Couldn't you at least leave me in the grave for three months before you start seeing another woman?"

Different people have different ideas about how to mourn, and for how long. But how can a person who's in mourning be blessed? The Bible promises not mourning, but happiness.

Nehemiah told people to stop mourning because the joy of the Lord is your strength.

> Then he said unto them, Go your way, eat the fat, and drink the sweet, and send portions unto them for whom nothing is prepared: for *this* day *is* holy unto our Lord: neither be ye sorry; for the joy of the LORD is your strength.
>
> —Nehemiah 8:10

Paul told the Thessalonians not to sorrow.

> But I would not have you to be ignorant, brethren, concerning them which are asleep, that ye sorrow not, even as others which have no hope.
>
> —1 Thessalonians 4:13

Solomon wrote that God's blessings make us rich and He adds no sorrow to them.

> The blessing of the LORD, it maketh rich, and he addeth no sorrow with it.
>
> —Proverbs 10:22

The prophet Isaiah said that sorrow and mourning shall flee away.

> Therefore the redeemed of the LORD shall return, and come with singing unto Zion; and everlasting joy *shall be* upon their head: they shall obtain gladness and joy; *and* sorrow and mourning shall flee away.
>
> —Isaiah 51:11

Don't these promises contradict this "blessing" Jesus talks about?

The Right Kind Of Mourning

The Bible promises that we will be joyful and happy, but it never promises that we will not go through seasons of mourning. It is natural to grieve the loss of a job, money, a friendship, a loved one, or damages wrought by your own sin or someone else's.

David mourned the loss of his baby by Bathsheba. Jesus mourned the loss of John the Baptist when he was beheaded. Abraham mourned for Sarah and wept for her.

In this second lesson, Jesus was saying not that happiness comes from constantly mourning, but rather that to be happy, you must express grief in the proper way.

There is a false teaching that says to turn your back on your sorrows. You might have heard people say, "Don't let this get you down. God doesn't want you to be sad about it. Be happy or you won't get victory." There is a knee-jerk reaction against sadness in our culture, as if it is an unacceptable emotion. People wear "Smile, God loves you!" buttons, and tell each other to cheer up and be a good sport. This is painfully obvious at some funerals where people try to make the family of the deceased happy, sometimes by reminding them that their loved one is with

Jesus. That may be true, but it doesn't take the place of healthy mourning.

Mourning isn't mourning unless it's expressed. In one of Billy Graham's books, he tells about Frances, a neighbor of Billy and Ruth's. Frances lost her husband to a tragic accident and thought she'd let the Lord down if she expressed any kind of sorrow. She put on a brave look and was cheerful all the time. Everybody thought she had the victory over sadness that only Jesus could give her, but really she bottled it all up on the inside.

One day Ruth called and there was no answer at Frances' home, so she went over and there was no answer at the door. Ruth went in and there was Frances, sitting in a chair, staring at the floor, drooling. Ruth said, "Frances, are you okay?" and Frances spoke in monosyllables. Ruth called the doctor, who immediately recognized the signs of suppressed grief. Only by owning up to her emotions was Frances able to return to normal living.

I read an amazing book that told about researchers who took the blood of normal, healthy, happy people and injected it into guinea pigs. Nothing happened. Then they took blood from people who had suppressed fears, unbearable frustration or constant anger. When they injected a couple of drops of this blood into the guinea pigs, the guinea pigs quickly died. Researchers identified recognizable poisons in the blood, created by the suppressed emotions.

Suppressing emotions is not the secret of happiness. Proper mourning must be expressed if we are to get past it. All of us have lost loved ones and have wept until our eyes burned. We have gone through every conceivable emotion, all the "What ifs" and "I should haves" until we come out the other side. Denying this process is denying our mind and body the chance to be free of sorrow.

Mourning For Sin

It is also healthy to mourn for our sin or for the sin of others. Jesus looked over Jerusalem and wept. In essence, He said, "Jerusalem, Jerusalem, God loves you, and He sent you prophets to show you the way, and you killed them. He sent you messengers and you stoned them. Now the Son of God has come to rescue His people, and you are rejecting Him." Jesus wept, not because He felt sorry for Himself for not being received, but because judgment was coming. He was grieved at the hard-heartedness of the people.

We, too, can mourn for the sin in our lives or in our nation. But there is a fine line between mourning and griping. I have heard some preachers who think they are mourning for America's sins when they are really griping about things they don't like. They are puffed up, not humble. I heard one preacher say, "I'm concerned about America. Instead of trust, I find lust. We're taking harlots and turning them into starlets." He was griping in rhyme! His mourning did nothing for America and was only a way to vent his own frustration at the culture around him.

There are other mistakes to avoid during the season of mourning which we will look at in the next chapter.

If you overdo your sorrow,
you can actually be
consumed by it.

Chapter Three

Blessed Are Those
Who Mourn Properly

Proper mourning is healthy. But grief that is over-expressed turns to worldly sorrow which drags on and on. The process of mourning should have a beginning, a middle and an end. One time I asked the Lord how long a person should mourn. I found an answer in Genesis 50:1-5 where it says that seventy days they mourned for the loss of a loved one. That is two months and ten days.

That is a good rule of thumb for us today. Beyond that, a person can develop a spirit of worldly sorrow which I believe puts them on a course toward more sorrow. They might start having accidents, injuries, or sicknesses because they embrace a spirit of unhealthy sorrow and view themselves as victims.

Peter, after he denied the Lord, wept bitterly. He mourned over his sin, and was restored. Judas felt sorry for himself, hopelessness gripped him and he took his life. He did not mourn, but picked up a spirit of grief.

I've met some people who carry a spirit of grief with them. They look solemn and want to share their story of grief with you.

But Jesus instructs us not to be like the Sadducees; of a sad countenance. In other words, don't mourn all the time. Paul said in Second Corinthians that if you overdo your sorrow, you can actually be consumed by it. A man in the Corinthian church was caught in sin and he repented, but the church was still treating him like he was a sinner. Paul said, in essence, "Receive him like a brother because this over-mourning is going to eat him up if you don't." (II Corinthians 2:7).

Sowing Seeds In Sorrow

Psalm 55 gives us a progression for sorrow. It starts out saying:

...for I am overwhelmed by my troubles.

—Psalm 55:2b (NTL)

But the psalmist ended, saying:

...but I will trust in thee.

—Psalm 55:23c

The psalmist began in sorrow but ended in joy. That should be our pattern. Mourning should eventually lead to joy. How? Jesus gave us the model during His darkest hour of mourning in the Garden of Gethsemane:

> Then saith he unto them, My soul is exceeding sorrowful, even unto death: tarry ye here, and watch with me.
>
> And he went a little further, and fell on his face, and prayed, saying, O my Father, if it be possible, let this cup pass from me: nevertheless not as I will, but as thou *wilt*.
>
> —Matthew 26:38-39

He did two things with His mourning:

• He prayed until victory and comfort came to Him.

• He got up from there and planted a seed — His own life.

Those are the two things we must do in mourning. First, pray until you get comfort. If you don't barricade your heart with prayer, the mourning will turn to griping and will attract a spirit of grief. That will lead you down the wrong road.

I hear some people grieve over their own sins, or the errancy of their children, but I never find them at prayer meetings. That kind of grieving is like a stalled engine. Grief must be prayed through, or it becomes something unhealthy.

The second thing is to plant a seed. I had lunch with a missionary evangelist shortly after he had experienced a serious tragedy. He was overseas ministering, when he received a phone call telling him that his wife had been killed in an accident. Immediately demons came against him with words like, "You should have been there. You were over here trying to win foreigners to the Lord, and your own wife is dead."

This missionary called his friend, Oral Roberts, and Oral said, "We went through grief when our daughter and her husband were killed in a jet crash. We could hardly stand to think of our little daughter spread out in that field, dead. Then God told us to plant a seed and to go on national television letting the whole nation see what we were going through. He said there are millions of people suffering hurt, and they don't know what to do about it."

Oral and Evelyn Roberts did just that, though they were in pain so intense that all they wanted was to hide away. They called in the television crew and taped a half-hour television program, and after the taping, a brand-new strength came to Oral and his wife, and they began to have a new vision of what God was going to do through the ministry.

My missionary friend followed Oral's advice and began by praying through for eight hours. He couldn't even think of anything to pray, so he prayed in the spirit. And at the end of eight hours, comfort came, strength came, and God showed him what seed to plant for a harvest blessing.

What does it mean to plant a seed? It means getting back in the saddle of ministry. It means giving of your time, money, or effort even when all you feel like doing is dying. It means sowing seeds into the Kingdom during the time of sorrow.

A Glimpse Of Hope

Evelyn Roberts, Oral's wife, wrote a little book called *Suicide: Double Grief* after the death of their oldest son, Ronnie. Ronnie was a brilliant man who spoke seven languages fluently, then went to Vietnam and saw pain and hurt and was overcome with sorrow and anger. He kept it inside, then started going to the doctor for depression and the doctor prescribed a medication, but it didn't work. He went to his mom and dad's house and said, "I want so badly to serve Jesus, but I'm so depressed." They prayed with him and he seemed to get victory, but one day his dead body was found in an abandoned car, with a gun sitting next to him.

Can you imagine Evelyn's pain? She gave birth to Ronnie, and he was her first son. She fed him, watched him learn to walk, took him to kindergarten, watched him play ball, and now he was gone in the cruelest way.

To make it worse, she had always been taught that when somebody commits suicide they go immediately to hell. She couldn't bear the thought of Ronnie burning in eternal torment. Oral said, "There's only one thing we can do. We're going to pray until comfort comes. Then we're going to get a word from God and plant a seed." They prayed until God spoke and said, "Oral, I want you to record the New Testament on cassette tape, and put your comments in as you go along. That's going to be your seed."

Planting a seed in a time of sorrow never sounds like a fun thing to do, but it is a test of perseverance. Then Evelyn said, "What's going to be my seed?" Oral said, "You're going to run the tape recorder for me." Evelyn had no technical training, but she agreed and something happened as she listened to her husband read through the Bible. She noticed that there was not one verse that said that if you commit suicide you will automatically go to hell. The seed she was planting had helped her gain a new perspective.

Then their friend Kenneth Hagin called and said, "Evelyn, I can't get this off of my heart. God has given me a word and I'm supposed to give it to you. First Corinthians 5:5 says to hand someone over to Satan, so that the sinful nature may be destroyed and his spirit saved on the day of the Lord. And God showed me this is what happened to Ronnie."

God gave her a glimpse of hope that her dead son would be waiting in Heaven for her.

Sowing a seed in sorrow always produces joy, and it also produces fruit in a ministry. I think of two ministers I know in Detroit who started a church in a former X-rated theater. They mourned those who had been led astray by the theater, but they did something more than that. They prayed and bought the theater and turned that community around. Today former addicts, prostitutes, homeless people, and men who used to attend the X-rated theater go to their thriving inner-city church.

Maybe you've had pain. Maybe you are in mourning even now. If you are praying and planting a seed, that mourning will bring blessing.

The key is balance. Let the season of mourning come and go. Ecclesiastes says there is a season for everything, including weeping and laughter. This doesn't mean you are failing if sadness returns periodically. Anyone who has seriously mourned knows that it often comes back, and you feel like you are going through it again, though in a more condensed way. That is natural. Talk with other people who have mourned, read books about it, and especially stay in God's Word for encouragement.

Avoid the extremes of under-expressing and over-expressing your pain. Don't deny it, but don't let it rule you. Pray it through and plant a seed, and happiness will come.

Chapter Four

Blessed Are
The Nonjudgmental

The Couches thought they had found the ideal place to live — a new home in a South Carolina neighborhood. It was two stories tall, with a big backyard. It sat on a clean, new street. They pictured raising their daughter there for many years, so they took out a mortgage and moved in.

But when Christmas rolled around, the problems began. While Lorinda Couch was out shopping five days before Christmas, a pipe froze and burst, flooding the house. She came home to find the Christmas tree on the floor and the packages floating in water. The pipes had not been insulated properly.

But what they didn't understand was why red mud was now in their home. The pipes were for clean water, but further inspection revealed that the carpet had been installed over dirt, and when the water soaked through, the dirt came out.

The Couches moved in with family in another state for ten days, then returned home to find that the home builder had used a sealant inside the house that was releasing poisonous gas. Their daughter began having coughing episodes, so they moved into a hotel until the builder came back and used a different sealant.

They returned to the house, where the furniture was stacked up on one side of the living room and the floor was stripped of carpet. They worked hard to get the place in livable condition, then noticed that the wood around the door was discolored due to water damage. Soon it started peeling up and breeding mold, and they realized that the front door was letting water in. So was the back door.

Then another pipe burst, this one in the ceiling. The plumber discovered mold where, unknown to them, the pipe had been leaking for some time.

The downstairs would not get warm, and the family had to huddle upstairs for breakfast and use a space heater to make the downstairs warm.

The clothes dryer would not work because the laundry room had not been wired. The windows to the backyard would not open.

And the structure itself was less than sturdy. They could push on one wall and make the entire house shake as if in a mild earthquake. The place was so drafty that the chandelier swung back and forth on windy days.

Today the Couches live in an apartment and are still making monthly mortgage payments on the house, which they deem unlivable. The front door leak has been repaired at least sixteen times, they say, and when the wind blows hard, the house threatens to collapse. They paid almost $130,000 for their home and estimate that it would take $170,000 just to fix it.

Real Estate

Can you imagine that happening to you? You might be tempted to throw up your hands and swear off ever buying a home or property again.

But property is exactly what Jesus promised in this next blessing:

> Blessed *are* the meek: for they shall inherit the earth.
>
> —Matthew 5:5

The word inherit means possess, obtain, or get by apportionment. "Earth" comes from the Greek word meaning soil, ground, or real estate. You might say, "Blessed are the meek, and as an added promise, they are going to be apportioned some real estate."

Real estate — except in extreme cases like the Couches' — is almost always a good investment. Even when the economy is sagging, real estate seems to hold its value.

How do we get it? In God's economy, you don't have to have a mortgage, a down payment, a home inspector, or a bank. You just have to learn to be meek.

That may not seem like a good trade because when we think of someone meek, we think of a doormat, someone who gets walked on, who takes insults with unlimited forbearance, who rolls over and plays dead.

I read a sales magazine that said, "The meek shall not inherit the Earth; they're going to have to buy it from the assertive." J. Paul Getty, the miserly oil baron, said, "The meek may inherit the Earth, but they're not getting the mineral rights!"

When God gives us real estate, we get everything right along with it, and there won't be any nightmares.

What Is Meekness?

It's too bad that "meek" rhymes with "weak," because they have totally different meanings. The

Bible gives no overt definition of the word meek, but neither does the Bible define concepts like holiness, though we know what they mean by the context they are used in and by what is considered their opposite.

The word picture given in the Bible for meekness is of a wild animal that has been domesticated for good use. A horse running around the plains does no good until he's broken, trained, and turned into a workhorse.

The opposite of meekness is rebellion. In Numbers 12, Moses' sister Miriam rebelled against Moses' authority and said, "Who does he think he is? He thinks God speaks only to him. We're all the people of God, so God can speak to us just like He speaks to Moses." God became upset with Miriam and struck her with leprosy. The Bible goes on to say that Moses was the meekest man in all the earth, so this passage contrasts meekness and rebellion.

Meekness is also the opposite of self-seeking, self-promoting, craving for honor, greedy, grasping, cocky, haughty, boastful and elbowing. It is the unselfish, gentle attitude of being strong in God, patient with people and sensitive to both God and man.

Meekness boils down to seven things. Let's look at them one at a time.

❑ **Number One: Meekness is realizing that you're imperfect, and so is everybody else.** A big part of meekness is in not judging people. In other words, give people a break. They're not perfect. You're not perfect. Let's find a way, through meekness of heart, to make our relationships work.

Moses realized that Miriam was imperfect. She was holding him to a higher standard than what she was willing to live up to, but what did Moses do? He prayed for her and asked God to heal her of leprosy. He accepted the imperfection and was meek in the face of her judging attitude.

A grandma and grandpa were married fifty years and the granddaughter asked the grandma how she had made it fifty years with grandpa. She said, "Before we got married, I decided to make a list of ten of his faults. I decided that after we got married, I would overlook those ten faults." The granddaughter asked what were the ten faults and Grandma said, "To tell you the truth, I never did get around to writing them down, so every time I saw a fault in your Grandpa, I said, 'That's one of the ten, and I'm going to overlook that.'"

That's a pretty good way to be meek!

A few years ago during a ministry trip, I took my wife, Mary Jo, to Paris for our anniversary. One of the interesting spots that we visited was the Cathedral of Notre Dame, a beautiful old structure. Every detail seemed perfect, but we noticed that the altar was a little bit off center. I later found out that they deliberately planned that imperfection because they wanted everybody to remember that nobody, and nothing is perfect, except God.

Keep a mental reminder like that in your head, so when you are tempted to judge somebody, you will have reason to back off.

☐ **Number Two: Meekness is being unselfish and unassuming.**

A young African man came to America to attend college. When he and other students were getting their room assignments, this man was the only one not fighting for the best room. He said, "If there's a room that nobody else wants, I'll take that." The man taking the requests was moved to tears because everybody else was so selfish, but this man had an unassuming manner. He was grateful to be in America, getting an education.

We need more churches like that, who say, "If there are people out there that nobody else wants, we'll take them." We need more people in the church who say, "If there's a job in the church that nobody else wants, I'll take that."

Chapter Five

Blessed Are
The Gentle And Gracious

Winston Churchill, one of the great leaders of the 20th century, led England to victory during World War II. At one time he had a spirit of meekness and gentleness, but after rising to fame he became self-centered and difficult to be around. If there was a traffic jam, he'd pull up on the sidewalk and drive along, and people would have to run to protect themselves.

One time Churchill got into an argument with a hotel valet and was yelling at this man, and the young man yelled back. Churchill replied, "How dare you yell at me," and the young man said, "You were yelling at me first." Churchill said, "Yes, but I'm great and you're not."

That kind of attitude eventually brought him down. His own people of England rejected him at the next election, and he became depressed and died a hurt man because he abandoned meekness.

☐ **Number Three: Meekness is being gentle and unobtrusive.**

This is a trait that Christians so often lack. Many times I meet self-designated prophets and prophetesses, and they have no gentleness about them. One of them grabbed me at the back door of our church and said, "Pastor Williams, I am a prophetess. There's going to be a terrible earthquake in Michigan." The earthquake never came, but this woman sent me many prophecies, and they were wacky, outrageous, and obtrusive. There was no gentleness about her spirit. I finally told her, "I believe you are a prophetess — a false prophetess." She sent me a prophecy predicting my imminent death! That, too, didn't happen.

If you're going to minister in the things of God, there needs to be gentleness and unobtrusiveness. Your manner must reflect what's in your heart — patience, and a willingness to not be the center of attention.

☐ **Number Four: Meekness is being sensitive and gracious to others.**

The world exalts the aggressive, the self-confident, the self-assertive, and the self-advertising person who stampedes his way to the top, no matter who gets hurt along the way.

But meekness is the opposite of those things. Robert Schuller told the story of three nuns who went to a baseball game. They sat down and a group of anti-Catholic men sat right behind them, and they decided they would insult the nuns. One of them said loudly, "I think I'm going to move to Texas. I hear there are very few Catholics there." Another said, "I'm going to Oklahoma. I hear there are even fewer Catholics there." The other said, "I think I'm going to Alaska, because I hear there aren't hardly any Catholics there."

Finally, one of the nuns turned around and said, "Why don't you all go to hell, because there aren't any Catholics there!"

That wasn't the most gracious response, but certainly the men were being insensitive. This aspect of meekness means we take care not to offend. Of course, there are times to offend people if God wants us to. Jesus offended the Pharisees all the time, and overturned the tables of the money changers in the temple. I bet they were offended at that!

But at other times, Jesus took care not to offend, such as when he told Peter to go look in a fish's mouth for tax money:

> Notwithstanding, lest we should offend them, go thou to the sea, and cast an hook, and take up the fish that first cometh up; and when thou hast opened his mouth, thou shalt find a piece of money: that take, and give unto them for me and thee.
>
> —Matthew 17:27

Meekness is being sensitive to the situation and to the people involved.

☐ **Number Five: Meekness is having a sensitive posture toward God.**

In Psalm 37, there are no less than five verses that promise the Earth to the meek, and if you distill them into one trait, it is having a sensitive posture toward God.

There was a senior surgeon in a major metropolitan hospital, and he had a survival rate higher than any other surgeon in the city. Interns and residents liked to work with him to find out his secrets. They noticed that before each surgery he would disappear for about ten minutes, and nobody would know where he was. Then he would reappear and go into surgery, and everything would go well.

One day they asked him where he went, and he said, "I realize that I'm an imperfect human being, that I don't know everything, and I've found that in surgery many times things come up that you don't expect, and you have to make split-second decisions that could cost a person his life. So I go into the janitor's closet and say, 'God, I'm just one man, and I want to have a sensitive heart toward You. I can't do this without You. Sometimes I need to make a decision and I want Your wisdom.' Then during the surgery answers will come to me."

What an example he set!

I can't tell you how much I appreciated it when I had shoulder surgery, and I was being wheeled into the recovery room. I remember a voice that said, "Pastor Dave, my name is Sally, I'm the recovery room nurse. Would you like me to pray with you?" I said, "Yes!" I don't remember the prayer, but I remember she prayed for me, and I remember how comforting it was to have somebody praying for me when I felt incapacitated.

That's having a sensitive posture toward God.

❑ **Number Six: Meekness is having a sensitive posture toward God's authority.**

A Roman centurion came to Jesus one time and said, "My servant needs healing." Jesus said, "I'll come and heal him," but the centurion said, "I'm a man with authority and I understand how this works. I say to one man, 'Go,' and he does. You just speak the word and my servant will be healed" (See Matthew 8:8-9).

This man recognized God's authority and was sensitive to it. Jesus healed his servant and said he had greater faith than anyone else in Israel.

We already looked at Miriam's mistake when she came against God's authority in Moses. There are many other examples too. King Saul lost his meekness, and it ruined him. David, on the other hand, had an opportunity to kill Saul and crown himself as king, but he wouldn't do it. He said he wouldn't dare touch the anointed of God.

Some churches are ruined because the church board doesn't have a sensitive posture toward God's authority. The board at my church is heavenly. They are always trying to bless me. One of my elders said they have noticed that whenever the church is facing a plateau or the finances are running a little low, they bless me with a gift and everything starts picking up again. I'm glad they noticed that!

Many churches have boards that are not meek, and that's why they are not getting any real estate. When people try to manipulate God-appointed authority, they forfeit this blessing.

We should respect the authority God puts in our lives. Women, respect the authority of your husbands. Men, respect the authority of Spirit-inspired words and ideas that come through your wife.

Respect the authority of God's Word, of a prophet, an apostle, a pastor, an evangelist, or a teacher. Respect anyone in elected office as governing at God's will.

❑ **Number Seven: Meekness is quiet resignation to the will of God.**

God wouldn't let Moses go into the Promised Land because Moses had sinned, and Moses could have fought with God but he didn't. He quietly followed the will of God, went up into the mountain and died, and God made him one of the greatest men who has ever lived.

Meekness is embodied in the Words of Jesus to His Father:

> ...nevertheless not as I will, but as thou *wilt*.
>
> **—Matthew 26:39c**

Beatitudes: Success 101

I knew a couple who had a messed-up marriage. The love, the spark, everything was gone. But they met Jesus, were filled with the Holy Spirit, and realized that the will of God was for them to make their marriage work, though neither one of them had the desire. Today they are happier than they ever dreamed. Meekness paid off!

A young preacher came to an older preacher and said, "I want to learn from you. Here's a list of my credentials." The young man rattled off his accomplishments while the old man continued to pour a cup of coffee, until the young man noticed that coffee was running over the sides of the cup. "Watch out!" he said, leaping back. The old preacher said, "I did that on purpose to make a point. When you come to me, you can't come with a full cup, or I can't put anything else in it. When you're ready to receive, then I can teach you."

When you come to God, you can't come with your own dreams, your own ambitions, your own aspirations, and ask Him to bless them automatically. You've got to say, "Let me know specifically what you have planned for my life." Then, in meekness, you follow His will.

To sum it up, meekness is:

1. Realizing that you're imperfect, and so is everyone else.

2. Being unselfish and unassuming.

3. Being gentle and unobtrusive.

4. Being sensitive and gracious to others.

5. Having a sensitive posture toward God.

6. Having a sensitive posture toward God's authority.

7. Quiet resignation to the will of God.

The more meek you are, the more God will bless you with a portion of His creation to oversee and tend.

In the next chapter, we'll look at everyone's favorite subject — a healthy appetite.

But Jesus says if you hunger after spiritual things it's going to be satisfying.

Chapter Six

Blessed Are Those Who Have A Spiritual Appetite

On a warm clear day at Brooklyn's famous Coney Island, 360-pound Ed "The Animal" Krachie bellied up to the table of the world's most famous hot-dog-eating contest. The crowd gathered around, and Ed scoped out his competition — several other massive Americans and a conspicuously tiny Japanese man named Hirofumi Nakajima who stood 5 feet 6 inches and weighed 135 pounds.

Krachie, the reigning champion, knew he had it made. He would mop the floor with the other contenders. The twelve-minute contest required each man to eat as many hot dogs (and buns) as he could. The reward: an International Mustard Yellow belt, a trophy and twenty pounds of hot dogs.

In a tense moment of stillness, the race began. Down the hatch went one hot dog after another, taking mere seconds to disappear. The men stood to get more leverage, stuffing them down their throats. One, two, three …

… eight, nine, ten …

… fourteen, fifteen, sixteen …

The final minute ticked off the clock, and Ed "The Animal" was sure he had retained his title. He thought of where he would put the belt and trophy in his Queens, New York, home. He awaited the praise of the crowd.

And then the judge called the winner: *Hirofumi Nakajima!*

The little Japanese man had eaten twenty-four hot dogs in twelve minutes. Stunned and confused, Ed conceded defeat, then went home to nurse his ego and plot his comeback.

It was the last time Ed would even come close to winning the hot-dog-eating title, and one of the last times an American would win. In subsequent years the title went to several other Japanese men, including one who weighed 101 pounds and set a record by consuming twenty-five hot dogs. Soon the event was dominated by the Japanese, one of whom also held the banana-eating record (twenty-six in twelve minutes).

Ed "The Animal" retired with one last comment: "I don't know where they put it. Both of those guys [the first and second place winners] put together weigh less than me."

Where did the skinny Japanese men get their appetite? Maybe they wanted the fame. After all, they traveled from Japan to New York just for the event.

Maybe they hungered after the trophy.

Whatever the reason, they showed the world a winning formula: You don't have to be the biggest, and you don't have to have the most intimidating reputation. You just have to have the biggest appetite!

Hungry For Righteousness

That contest is a picture of the kind of hunger Jesus wants us to have for righteousness.

> Blessed *are* they which do hunger and thirst after righteousness: for they shall be filled.
>
> —Matthew 5:6

In fact, hunger for righteousness is required for someone to understand the very blessings Jesus talks about. A simple reading of the Sermon on the Mount would provide no revelation into the true meaning of what Jesus was saying. He said to the disciples, "It has been given to you to know the secrets of the Kingdom." Why? Because they had a spiritual appetite.

When Mother Theresa visited the United States, she made an observation. She said, "In India, people are dying of physical hunger, but in America, people are dying of spiritual hunger."

Sometimes we hunger after things that don't satisfy:

- Fame

- Success

- Power

- Prestige

- Popularity

- Money

- Cars

- Houses

One man promised to be happy after he got his own home. Then he said he'd be happy after he got a vacation home. Then a speedboat. Then a third car. Then a yacht. The hunger for things never seems to satisfy. It's like looking in the full refrigerator when you're hungry, but nothing sounds good.

But Jesus says if you hunger after spiritual things, namely righteousness, you're going to be filled. It's going to be satisfying.

Jesus fasted for forty days and then was hungry. The devil came to Him on the Mount of Temptation in Jericho and said, "If you're really the Son of God, take these rocks and turn them into bread." Jesus made an amazing statement:

> It is written, Man shall not live by bread alone, but by every word that proceedeth out of the mouth of God.
>
> —Matthew 4:4

It is more important to have a spiritual appetite than to have a physical appetite. We can live for quite a while without food, but we can't live long without water. Most people would last no more than about three days without water. The longest time a person went without water in contemporary times is about ten days.

And yet food and water are not the most important things, eternally speaking. God's Word is.

When I required surgery on my broken shoulder, the doctor instructed me not to eat or drink after midnight the day before the surgery. I didn't think it would be a problem, but when I got up in the morning, the first inclination was to get a drink of water. I was thirsty, but I had to stop myself before I put the glass to my lips. I wanted water so bad! I checked into the hospital, and it took awhile for them to prepare me for surgery. My body was screaming for water. I asked if they could give me an ice chip, but they said, "Sorry, Mr. Williams — no water."

How desperate I felt! My body started to feel hot and weak, my stomach soured, my mouth and eyes were dry and achy.

When I woke up from surgery, I felt as though all the water had drained out of me. A nurse brought me a cup of water, and when I drank it I felt like each drop was being soaked up by my body like a dry sponge. I don't think I've ever felt such physical relief!

That experience gave me a new appreciation for what true thirst is. It's not waiting an extra half-hour to get a drink. It's listening to your stomach and the rest of your body beg for nourishment.

In Israel I saw the Bedouin people who are nomadic and live in the wilderness with flocks of camels and sheep. The patriarch decides when to move camp, and they'll go twenty or thirty miles away and set up their tents, but they have to go where there's water. If they don't find water, they have to kill a camel and cut the liver out because there's liquid in the liver that will sustain their life for another two or three days. I'm sure there have been times when even the liver water ran out.

This thirst that Jesus speaks about is a thirst which makes you feel like you're going to die if you don't get something to drink. Our walk with Christ takes us through several types of thirst. First we thirst for Jesus to save us, realizing that we cannot save ourselves. Once that happens, we have another thirst; to be more like the One who saved us. That is the thirst for righteousness.

How do we develop a spiritual appetite? Let's look at the answers in the next chapter.

We search for relief, try different plans, list twelve moral principles that we're going to live by, but there's only one way to find real relief.

Chapter Seven

Blessed Are The Truly Righteous

My family and I were in Israel visiting the Mount of Temptation, when we decided to go to the restaurant at the bottom of that mountain, called the Temptation Restaurant. It was a buffet-style place, and it was very busy. My wife, Mary Jo, and my daughter, Trina, made it through the line and were seated, but my son, David, and I got stuck between a bunch of people.

Then the lady behind me started pushing and shoving us to get to the food she wanted. She was easily the rudest person I've ever seen in my life. She reached right over our trays and spooned food onto her plate, and her elbows got in my food. David said to me, "I know why this is called the Temptation

Restaurant, because I'm being tempted to belt that woman!"

I had the same temptation, but my name badge said "Pastor Dave Williams," so I had to behave!

That woman, for whatever reason, was not behaving righteously. Righteousness is to be right with God, right with yourself, and right with others. Let me share three things that righteousness is not, to get rid of any misconceptions that may surround the word.

❏ **Number One: Righteousness is not self-righteousness.**

Self-righteousness means believing that your works or good character are enough to make you a good person. The Gospel of Jesus Christ does promote righteousness, but never does it promote self-righteousness.

I was eating in a Chinese restaurant one time and a lady came up to me and said, "Aren't you Pastor Williams? I've watched your television program for a long time, and now I've started coming to your church. It's such a blessing to me." I thanked her, and she sat down at a nearby table. After I finished my meal, the server brought me a fortune cookie. I opened it and read the slip of paper inside. The woman who had paid me the compliment looked over at me, saw the fortune cookie and said, "I can't believe that a pastor would read a fortune in a fortune cookie!"

She went from sweet to self-righteous in about five seconds! Apparently I wasn't as righteous as she was.

Self-righteousness comes whenever we think we have accomplished something on our own.

> I am the vine, ye *are* the branches: He that abideth in me, and I in him, the same bringeth forth much fruit: for without me ye can do nothing.
>
> —John 15:5

> Except the LORD build the house, they labour in vain that build it: except the LORD keep the city, the watchman waketh *but* in vain.
>
> —Psalms 127:1

> We are so glad that we can say with utter honesty that in all our dealings we have been pure and sincere, quietly depending upon the Lord for his help and not on our own skills. And that is even more true, if possible, about the way we have acted toward you.
>
> —2 Corinthians 1:12 (TLB)

> We dare to say these good things about ourselves only because of our great trust in God through Christ, that he will help us to be true to what we say, and not because we think we can do anything of lasting value by ourselves. Our only power and success comes from God.
>
> —2 Corinthians 3:4-5 (TLB)

In Jerusalem, Jews still gather by the thousands at the Western Wall, many of them wearing phylacteries, little boxes that contain the Commandments of God, on their forehead so their eyes can constantly see it, because the Bible says to keep God's Word ever before your eyes. They are hoping to attain some kind of righteousness by spending hours praying at the Western Wall.

That is not what Jesus meant by righteousness.

❑ **Number Two: Righteousness is not an incurable compulsion to be holy.**

People who are constantly striving and working toward some degree of holiness are miserable, and they want everybody else to be miserable. Martin Luther was that way before he led the Protestant Reformation. He would walk for miles on his knees, his knees bleeding from sharp stones on the road, thinking that this asceticism was making him righteous. And then one day, Luther read the books of Romans and Galatians where it says the just shall live by faith, and he realized that he had confused self-effort with righteousness. He left his works behind and embraced a righteousness that was not of himself.

But others are still trapped in the compulsion to make themselves holy. One monk near Jericho made a vow at a young age to never see or speak to another human being. He found a cave in a mountain shaft and went to live there. He's an old man now and has lived there for decades. They put food down to him once a day in a bucket and he sends his waste material back up. Why? He is trying to attain righteousness or holiness.

He should have looked more closely at the life of Jesus who didn't hide out to show us how to live holy. In fact, he didn't even hang around the righteous people, but the unrighteous.

Righteousness is not about making ourselves holy. Only God can make us holy. Our job is to have the appetite for it.

☐ **Number Three: Righteousness is not trying to measure up to someone else's religious standard.**

When someone imposes their religious standard on people — a standard Jesus never intended — it makes them slaves. The woman at the Chinese restaurant who chided me for looking inside a fortune cookie wanted me to live up to her standard. In reality, there's only one standard to live up to: absolute, one hundred percent perfection. Jesus said:

> For I say unto you, That except your righteousness shall exceed *the righteousness* of the scribes and Pharisees, ye shall in no case enter into the kingdom of heaven.
>
> —Matthew 5:20

That's a hard standard, but it's possible by letting God's righteousness come upon us. There are five stages to this:

• **Stage One:** God reveals His perfect standard for our lives.

• **Stage Two:** We begin to feel thirsty and hungry for righteousness, but also frustrated in our pursuit of it. Isaiah 64:6 says that any righteousness we can muster up is like throwing oily, dirty, garbage-filled rags before God.

• **Stage Three:** We become conscious of our guilt before God.

I went on a prayer retreat years ago to cleanse myself of my hidden faults. I started making a list of my wrong attitudes and secret sins, thinking I would have five or six, but before I knew it I had a legal-size page filled up. I started on the second page, and that one filled up, too, so I ripped them apart and said, "God, I can't do it! I'm a mess! Why did you call me to preach? Surely there's somebody more righteous, more holy, and more godly than me." I had reached a point of acknowledging my guilt.

• **Stage Four:** We search for relief, try different plans, list twelve moral principles that we're going to live by every day. But there's only one way to find real relief for this hunger for righteousness, and that's by ceasing from our own justifying (no more, "God, I wouldn't have yelled at my wife if she hadn't ..."). Then we abandon all pretense of personal righteousness. We take off the mask and quit pretending that we've done so many good things that it certainly outweighs the bad.

Then we take a place in the dust before God, bowing before His righteousness. That dust in the face will make you thirsty!

• **Stage Five:** God becomes our righteousness so that sin is no longer counted against us.

> Yes, what joy for those whose record the LORD has cleared of sin...
>
> —Psalms 32:2 (NLT)

We find ourselves clothed with righteousness. It's not ours but His, purchased on the Cross.

The Reward: Being Filled

When we allow God's righteousness to clothe us, the Bible says we are filled, fed, satisfied, supplied in abundance. The word picture of filled means a fruitful, well-irrigated garden, overflowing with luscious fruits and vegetables. What happens when we quit trying to attain righteousness, and start hungering and thirsting after righteousness? God makes you like a garden that grows beautiful fruit. People will look at you and see beauty. He will take away the factory kind of spiritual existence where we punch in, work hard for God, sweat, pour the molten metal, then punch out, and He'll turn that factory into a garden — peaceful, relaxing, fresh, fragrant.

That's the reward for having a spiritual appetite!

Next, let's look at what it means to help others get out of bad situations.

Chapter Eight

Blessed Are The Merciful

Jesus laid out His Success 101 course strategically, giving it a natural order and progression.

• Poor in spirit — That's when we discover that we are nothing and can do nothing apart from Jesus Christ.

• Mourning — We have a godly sorrow for sins and learn to mourn in a healthy way.

• Meekness — We become sensitive and gracious toward others and resign ourselves to God's will.

• Spiritual hunger — We begin to develop a spiritual appetite.

Now we come to a beautiful attitude that teaches us how to sow into other people's lives.

> Blessed *are* the merciful: for they shall obtain mercy.
>
> —Matthew 5:7

A pastor was driving to church one day, late for service. A police officer pulled him over for speeding, and as the officer approached the pastor's window the pastor thought he would use the Bible to get out of the fine. He said, "Officer, the Bible says blessed are the merciful, for they shall obtain mercy." The officer handed him the ticket and said, "It also says, 'Go and sin no more.'"

The pastor didn't get the kind of mercy he wanted that day!

When someone sacrifices something important to them in order to help a fellow suffering creature, that's one form of mercy. There was a true story about a mutt who set an example for mercy. The dog's owner noticed one day that the dog didn't seem to be eating much. He fed the dog scraps from the table, and the dog put as much as he could put in his mouth and walked into the woods. This went on for a few days, and the owner wondered where he was going. One day he fed the dog scraps and the dog put everything into his mouth and walked out into the woods, but this time the owner followed him. There he found another dog trapped in barbed wire. His dog had been taking food to him every day.

Mercy is one of the most beautiful lessons we can learn because it's an attribute of God Himself. The Bible tells us that it's a very large part of God's character and nature. He said He would rather show mercy than bring judgment.

He's merciful to the backslider who returns, to sinners who repent, to orphans and widows. This doesn't just mean that He offers them salvation. That's grace, not mercy. There is a difference. Grace is when God forgives our sins. Mercy is when he lifts us out of the misery and consequences and suffering that sin brought.

Showing Mercy

Mercy is a characteristic of genuine disciples. I get concerned about ministers who crucify other ministers when they fall. If we Christians don't show mercy in this world, who will?

Proverbs says that the righteous man is even merciful to his animals. He feels the miseries of their suffering and seeks to relieve them, even if it's that person's fault that he or she is suffering. It causes us to deal leniently with those who bring misery on themselves.

Jesus told the story about the servant who was shown mercy by the king, but who refused to show mercy to a fellow servant. Instead of choosing the path of mercy, he chose the path of revenge (Matthew 18:23-35).

There is nothing more miserable than a person who is eaten alive by revenge. I think of the prophet Hosea in the Bible. He married a lady named Gomer, and they had two boys and a girl — a happy family. But Gomer didn't like being in the ministry. She wanted the fun life and started fooling around and finally slipped into prostitution and started selling her body to any man who could pay the price.

But she was the one who paid a price. She had become old fast. Her face began to wrinkle, her eyes began to sag, and she couldn't make as much money selling herself as she once did. Finally her pimp sold her as a slave. She hadn't seen her husband in years, knew nothing about her children, and now her life was wasted.

She was put on the auction block, and the auctioneer said, "I'm going to sell this woman to the highest bidder. She can wash dishes, she can do laundry, and she can scrub floors. She's not beautiful anymore; she's all worn out, but she can do some work." People started bidding on her.

Two dollars ...

Four dollars ...

Six dollars …

Going once, going twice.

Then somebody jumped up and said, "I'll give you two thousand dollars for her." There in the crowd was Hosea, buying back his wife. She did not deserve it, but he was moved by mercy.

When We Don't Deserve It

We all want to experience that kind of mercy, and we all can, because the God we serve is constantly reaching out to us with mercy. I knew a couple who got into a home business that promised to make them wealthy. They invested all of their money, but after a few months realized it was a fraudulent business. Now they had lost their savings and weren't able to pay their phone, light, or gas bill. The electricity went off, the gas went off, and they were threatened with eviction.

It would be easy to say that they deserved it because they should have recognized a scam when they saw one. After all, the Bible says the person who wishes to get rich quick will quickly become poor. But mercy moved in to alleviate their suffering.

A Christian couple in their neighborhood found out about their situation and took up an offering to pay their bills. They also invited them to a Bible study. How can you not come to a Bible study when they paid your bills and kept you from being evicted?

As a result, the man and woman accepted Jesus, started coming to church and were baptized. They became terrific disciples of Jesus Christ, because somebody showed them mercy.

Psalm 109 contains a prophecy regarding Judas Iscariot. It says in verse 16:

> **Because that he remembered not to shew mercy, but persecuted the poor and needy man...**

Judas didn't remember mercy. In fact, he was the one that was griping about giving money to the poor. The psalm foretold his end:

> **As he loved cursing, so let it come unto him: as he delighted not in blessing, so let it be far from him.**
>
> **—Psalm 109:17**

If you want mercy to be close to you, show mercy to others. You will reap a host of benefits, which we'll talk about in the next chapter.

Chapter Nine

Blessed Are
The Mercy Givers

There are four benefits to showing mercy to others. Let's take a look at them.

☐ Number One: We will receive mercy ourselves.

A lady came to her pastor complaining, "My husband never compliments me anymore. Whenever he says anything to me it's a criticism. The food is never good enough. The laundry doesn't get done fast enough. Can't I do anything right?"

The pastor said, "When was the last time you gave a compliment to your husband?" She thought a moment and said, "I've only been worried about him complementing me. I haven't been thinking that much about complementing him." She started complementing him, showing mercy instead of anger, and soon he fell in love with her all over again and began to treat her like a royal princess.

We all need mercy, so we ought to give mercy. Mercy revitalizes relationships better than anything. Try it!

☐ Number Two: You will be honored.

> He that followeth after righteousness and mercy findeth life, righteousness, and honour.
>
> —Proverbs 21:21

As you are merciful, your reputation will begin to rise like a hot-air balloon. You will ascend to a place of honor in your community. Even the dog who showed mercy was honored with a big story in the papers, and now he is admired all over America.

Will any less happen to you?

☐ Number Three: You will be happy.

> ...he that hath mercy on the poor, happy *is* he.
>
> —Proverbs 14:21b

You know how good it feels to give to the needy. It gives you that warm, satisfied glow knowing you have helped God touch another life.

☐ Number Four: Your soul will be nourished.

> The merciful man doeth good to his own soul...
>
> —Proverbs 11:17a

That means you can actually "feed" your soul, building it up in maturity and strength by showing mercy.

How To Do It

How do we show mercy?

First, we do it with cheerfulness. Anything we give; whether possessions, or honor, or forgiveness, or mercy should be done willingly and with joy.

Second, we do it without holding a grudge. We don't lord it over someone by saying, "You got yourself into this mess, but I guess I'll get you out."

More than twenty years ago Tony Orlando had a hit song, "Tie a Yellow Ribbon Round the Old Oak Tree," that was based on a true story. Near Jacksonville, Florida, lived a man who had not been good to his wife and two kids, but she was very faithful to him. He started smoking marijuana, then started stealing things, and one day he robbed a bank, was caught, and was sentenced to twelve years in prison.

Statistics show that nearly every time a man goes to jail, his wife divorces him, but this man felt genuine remorse. He told his wife, "I've got twelve years to go until I'm out. I've been terrible to you, and I don't want the kids knowing that their dad went to prison. Don't ever write to me and I won't write to you. Find another man, one who will treat you good."

He was taken to prison, and she never wrote to him and he never wrote to her. After almost three years, he was paroled for good behavior. He had always wondered what kind of man his wife had found, and if she was doing okay. He wrote to her a week before he was released from prison and said, "I'm getting out of prison in a week. By now you've probably found somebody else. I know that I've treated you bad, but I thought I'd write you this one letter to see if you still love me, and maybe there's still a chance that we can have a home together. If you still want me, tie a yellow ribbon around the old oak tree in front of the house."

He took a bus to Jacksonville, and three young teenagers were on the bus with him. They noticed he was sad so they asked why and he related the story to them. "I don't know what I'm going to find," he said. "I don't know if my wife even still lives in this house, I haven't seen my kids in three years. I told her to tie a yellow ribbon around the old tree if she still wanted me."

The bus drew closer to where he used to live and as they turned down the street, the teenagers' faces were pressed against the window, looking to see if there was a yellow ribbon. The man was afraid to look. Suddenly it came into view and the teenagers started yelling for joy.

There was a yellow ribbon around the oak tree, a yellow sheet around the oak tree, and yellow pieces of cloth hanging all over it, and even bananas. Everything yellow she could find was on that oak tree. She was welcoming him back with open arms.

No, he didn't deserve to have his family back, but he discovered what mercy was all about.

That's the same attitude we should have when we show mercy. Take a chance. Give up whatever right you have to hold a grudge. Help someone out of a jam, and you, too, will receive mercy as Jesus promised.

A pure heart is what God wants us to have. He blesses people who are pure and promises that they will see Him.

Chapter Ten

Blessed Are
The Pure In Heart

Years ago I asked my son, David, to wash the windows on the house. He got a rag and some Windex and started rubbing them from the inside, but noticed they weren't getting any cleaner. He went outside and washed off the other side — but the windows didn't get any cleaner. He could see the smudges and the dirt, but he couldn't get them off.

He tried putting more Windex on the rag. He tried rubbing harder. Finally, he came to me in frustration, and I told him the problem: we had double insulated windows with the space of air between them, and no matter how much Windex he used on the outside and how hard he rubbed, the windows were still going to have smudges on the inside.

That's an illustration of our next blessing which says:

> **Blessed *are* the pure in heart: for they shall see God.**

—Matthew 5:8

Many people work hard to clean the outside of their life, putting on a better appearance, trying to make themselves better through education, culture, cosmetics, exercise, fashion, health clubs, tanning salons, even plastic surgeons. That may not be all bad, but fixing the outside never fixes the inside.

I read a Christian tract one time called *Thirty-six Do's and Don'ts Now That You Are a Christian.* It was given to the new converts in a church, and it told them how to dress, how to talk, who to make friends with, what music to listen to, what entertainment was okay. The whole message was based on exterior cleanup.

Maybe you've encountered people like that in the church who want to push their version of outer purity. That is not how Jesus did things. He went after the smudges on the inside of the window pane. He told the Pharisees that they had it all wrong because they cleaned the outside of the cup, but left the inside filthy.

> **For out of the heart proceed evil thoughts, murders, adulteries, fornications, thefts, false wit-**

ness, blasphemies: These are *the things* which
defile a man...

—Matthew 15:19-20

God wants us to have pure hearts. Purity relates
to holiness. It is a crystal-clear, brilliant word that almost defies human description. It means to be free
from any adulterant: unmixed, undiluted, free of de-
fects and contaminants. It implies absolute singleness:
without hypocrisy, cleansed, undivided. The bibli-
cal word picture for purity describes an unfolded
piece of cloth with nothing hidden in the folds or
pleats. In other words, "Blessed are those who have
an unfolded heart with no creases, no folds and nothing hidden."

Revelation 21:27 says only the clean and unde-
filed will enter into the Kingdom.

Nothing evil will be permitted in it—no one
immoral or dishonest—but only those whose
names are written in the Lamb's Book of Life.

—Revelation 21:27 (TLB)

Follow peace with all *men*, and holiness, without which no man shall see the Lord.

—Hebrews 12:14

Psalm 51, a monument to purity, says:

Create in me a clean heart, O God; and renew a
right spirit within me.

—Psalm 51:10

David knew that purity was an imperative with God.

Wrong Ways To Purity

There are a couple of false concepts about how to change people and make them better and purer. I've heard the phrase, "Change the environment and you'll change the man." But America and many other countries have tried to build good citizens, even launching programs like the Great Society and the War on Poverty. These changed the social environment somewhat, but people didn't change one bit! No legislated environmental change can bring purity of heart. Even Adam and Eve had the perfect environment, and they still went wrong.

Another false concept is, "Educate the man and you'll change the man." This has been disproved many times. The Romans were highly educated people, but the more educated they got, the more depraved they became until they became notorious for their love of violence in the Coliseum, their gluttony (they would hold food binges and people would go into a room called a vomitorium to expel the contents of their stomachs so they could continue eating), and their unleashed sexual promiscuity.

Germany, too, was a highly educated nation, but they put Adolph Hitler in charge. Saul, before he became the apostle Paul, was an educated Pharisee with the equivalent of several doctoral degrees, and yet he persecuted Christians.

Even today in America we are becoming simultaneously more educated and more addicted to impurity. Education doesn't change the heart, neither does the environment.

And yet, a pure heart is what God wants us to have. He blesses people who are pure and promises that they will see God. That sends shivers down my spine! It is my greatest desire to see God in the situations of life, to see Him working in me when I have a problem. I want to see Him in my times of joy, in my times of trouble, in my prayer closet and in the sanctuary. When my life is over, I want to see God face to face, without shame.

Christians with a pure heart can see God in a sense that nobody else can, both now and in the age to come. How do we develop this most precious trait? Let's find out in the next chapter.

God puts a bubble of protection around us that we only need to replenish with regular trips to His Word.

Chapter Eleven

Blessed Are
Those Who Pursue Purity

A few years ago I went through a struggle that made me wonder if I was doing the right thing with my life. The church I pastored had plateaued in its growth, and I wondered if I should move on and become a missionary or an evangelist. My heart was clouded with confusion.

I attended a conference at Oral Roberts University and was sitting in the lobby when a lady walked up to me and said, "I don't know who you are, but God spoke to me and told me to give you a message. There is a bright plan and a great future ahead. Don't stop what you're doing. Hang in there, be tenacious, God's going to see you through."

I looked at her, stunned, and thought, "Who is this woman? Has she been listening to me while I'm praying?" But my heart felt free of confusion for the first time in weeks. It had been purified by a fresh word, a coal from the fire of God.

Right after that incident I went out to lunch and as I drove through a green light, a man smashed his car into me and injured my shoulder. The pain was intense, but my first response was to praise God rather than complain. I realized that my heart was sending up praise because God had purified it.

That is often how purity comes: God intervenes to accomplish what we can't. When Isaiah saw the Lord in a vision he realized the depth of his impurity.

> "Woe *is* me!...for I am undone; because I *am* a man of unclean lips..."
>
> —Isaiah 6:5

But it was God who sent the angel to touch Isaiah's lips with a hot coal. We cannot possibly purify ourselves, but we can put ourselves in the path of purity. How?

❏ Number One: Intimacy with God and His Word.

God is able to keep us from getting dirty in a dirty world.

There was a coal mining town in Kentucky, and a fellow from the city visited and noticed that everything was sooty and had a gray hue to it from coal dust, except for one patch of brilliant white flowers. Astonished, he touched the flower petal and felt that it was covered with a natural oil that shed the coal dust.

That's what intimacy with God can do for us. We become Teflon-coated with the armor of God!

> **Wherewithal shall a young man cleanse his way? by taking heed *thereto* according to thy word.**
>
> **—Psalm 119:9**

I have a strange habit of studying spiders and snakes. I read about a water spider that has an amazing ability to keep itself alive under the water. It comes to the surface of the water, makes a bubble of air that fits around its body, then descends to the bottom of the pond where it is able to breathe amidst all the muck and slime. It stays there until the air runs out, then it resurfaces, builds another bubble and dives back down.

Isn't that like our lives? We work out where it's dirty and mucky, with people slandering each other, hanging up lewd posters, cursing God, and fighting their way to the top, and we wonder if it will rub off on us. But God puts a bubble of protection around us that we only need to replenish with regular trips to His Word.

One time I was visiting the lake with my family, and I had just started understanding that purity and holiness are things we should pursue. I was getting ready to go fishing, and all of a sudden I heard, "Holiness." I thought, "What does that mean? Is it wrong to go fishing?" I started getting my gear together to go fishing, and I heard it again. I said, "Lord, are you trying to tell me something?" Then it occurred to me that I hadn't bought a fishing license.

I resisted the idea of buying one and kept packing my gear, but then I heard it again — "Holiness." I got into the car, went to the bait shop and paid the money to buy a fishing license, and though I only caught a few baby fish, I felt so pure inside.

On that same trip, we were driving home and I was going seventy miles an hour, when the speed limit was fifty-five. All of a sudden I heard it again — "Holiness." I thought, "I don't want to go fifty-five!" So I compromised and slowed down to sixty-two. I heard it again — "Holiness." Finally I caved in and slowed down to fifty-five and set the cruise control. A few minutes later a state trooper pulled onto the highway right behind me. Purity paid off!

❑ **Number Two: Submit to the Refiner's fire.**

This is the part I don't care too much for. Who enjoys being burned?

> And he shall sit *as* a refiner and purifier of silver...
>
> —Malachi 3:3a

The Bible describes us often as God's silver and gold, and that sounds nice until we realize that the only way to purify them is with fire!

A Bible study group decided to visit a silversmith and watch him work. He showed them the silver ore that was his raw material, and he began to heat it until it melted. They asked him, "Why do you sit and watch the silver? Can't you go do something else until it melts?" He said, "I have to watch every moment because if the heat gets too hot, it will destroy the quality of the silver, and if it's not hot enough, all the dross won't come out."

That is how God refines us. He gets the heat hot enough to flush out the impurities, but not so hot that we are destroyed. But that wasn't all. The group asked how he knew the silver was purified, and the silversmith said, "When I can see my reflection in it." They realized that God is purifying us so that He can see His reflection.

The point of pursuing purity is to reflect Jesus more — to give Him a shiny surface so that people look at us and see Him! Be pure and you *will* see God. That's a promise!

Let's look at the lesson that turns you and me into everyday heroes.

Chapter Twelve

Blessed Are The Peacemakers

I've always dreamed of being a hero and emerging in some dire situation to save the day. I'm an amateur pilot, and every time I get on a commercial airplane, I remember a movie I saw years ago where the pilot and the co-pilot passed out, and the stewards had to find somebody to land the plane. A person who had never flown before volunteered and landed the airplane as the controller talked him down, and he was the hero of the movie.

I never want my plane to go down, but if it does, I wouldn't mind being the one who rescues it!

If you've ever dreamed about being a hero, this next lesson from Jesus is for you.

> Blessed *are* the peacemakers: for they shall be
> called the children of God.
>
> —Matthew 5:9

There are no greater heroes than people who make peace. Unfortunately, you don't see many statues built to peacemakers. Statues are built to war heroes, generals, men on horses.

Peace is appealing, but war is the rule. A statistician recently made a list of every war that had been fought in all of recorded history, and he discovered that there have been 14,531. That's about three per year. If you are forty years old, you've lived through 120 wars!

War is dehumanizing, whether it takes place in a family, a church, a company, or among nations. It causes us to look at other people as enemies and demons rather than fellow human beings.

How many times have you looked at your husband or wife, or brother or sister in the midst of a heated battle of wills and seen them as the enemy? It happens all the time in homes on your street and mine.

It happened in the Bible too: Cain and Abel, Isaac and Ishmael, Jacob and Esau. War goes back to the beginning.

How often does your workplace feel like trench warfare? Employees plot against the management and bad-mouth them among themselves. Management plots against employees, making strict rules and a toxic work environment. Employees fight other employees for benefits and promotions.

Even Christians fight each other. People often call and want to schedule meetings with me so they can dispute some part of my doctrine.

I was at a Christian conference one time, and outside the building was a man wearing a sandwich board that said, "Catholics are not Christians." His whole purpose was to divide people. I find that bullies and fight-pickers have a defective Christianity and insist on making judgments. Jesus said not to pull out the weeds, because you might get wheat as well.

"Peace, Man"

Jesus did not say blessed are the pacifists, but the peacemakers. Pacifists use this Scripture to justify their political or social stance, but pacifism isn't peacemaking. Sometimes it's the opposite. I well remember the hippies from the sixties who always said, "Peace, man," but recently I learned there is a new generation of hippies. I met some in a city I was visiting because they were staying in the same hotel as me. There were nine young people crammed into one room, and the room smelled heavily of body odor. I talked with one of them and he said, "We're here for a rock concert. We're on our way there right now." It was only nine in the morning, but they wanted to get there early!

I don't mind hippies, and I had hippie friends back when hippies were new, but I have noticed that they aren't particularly blessed in the way the Bible says. They tend to wander from place to place and have an idealized picture of the world. Sometimes they are trapped in poverty.

The Bible says blessed are the peacemakers, not the pacifists. How do we become peacemaking heroes? Let's take a look.

Chapter Thirteen

Blessed Are Those Who Bring Peace

I want to give you five steps to becoming a peace-maker so you can lay hold of this promise to be called a child of God.

☐ **Number One: Be at peace yourself.**

Have you known people who are fidgety? Uncomfortable? Conflicted inside themselves? Often it means they don't know the Prince of peace, so they don't have peace themselves.

Knowing Jesus is the starting point to becoming a peace hero. He is the God of all peace.

I said earlier, there are not many statues built to peace heroes, but there is one statue built to a peace hero in the Andes Mountains between Argentina and Chile. In 1899 Chile and Argentina were having a dispute and were ready to go to war, but a Chilean Christian man thought about all the hundreds and thousands of fathers who wouldn't come home to their children if they went to war. He began to talk about peace, and finally, miraculously, he got an audience with King Edward the Seventh, and asked if he would intervene to help them avoid war.

King Edward got involved and came up with a perfect solution that they hadn't seen before. War was averted. They took the unused guns from the Argentine and Chilean armies, melted them down and built a colossal statue of Jesus Christ with His arms outstretched, one arm toward Chile, and the other arm toward Argentina as a symbol that there is one real peacemaker and that is Jesus Christ.

And yet some Christians are not at peace with themselves. Why do people lose peace?

• *They want affirmation or recognition.* People's appreciation is fickle and fleeting. I learned a long time ago that one Sunday I may be a hero, and the next Sunday I may be a lightning rod for criticism. If you are looking for appreciation all of the time, that robs you of peace.

• *"Good enough" becomes an acceptable standard.* When we slide toward mediocrity, letting our potential drain away unused, it robs us of peace. If you ever say, "I'm a good enough husband, a good enough father. I do good enough work," you know you are inviting inner turmoil. God didn't create us to be "good enough," but to live up to our greatest potential of excellence. When we don't, it causes strife that comes from God to prod us to do our best.

• *They choose immediate pleasure over future personal growth.* I had a choice one time of going to another church for more money. At the time, I was an intern pastor making only $125 a week which wasn't even good pay in 1980. Another church asked me to come for $375 a week, but I turned them down because the weekly paycheck was less important than what I felt God speaking to my heart.

Chasing money robs you of peace. Learn to say, "It's enough," and be at peace with what He gives you.

• *They try to carry too heavy a load.* Imagine that your life is a bridge spanning two mountains. The mountain behind you represents your past, and the one in front of you is the future. The bridge itself is the day God has given you to live in. Some people want to carry 10,000 tons of rock and debris from their past life over the bridge, though the bridge can only hold 5,000 tons.

Others try to pull future burdens onto the bridge. Have you ever had a day that seemed to pile up on you? Your stomach churns, the tasks come in from the right and left, and you start worrying about the to-do list. Part of the problem is that you are trying to pull the future into the present, making the bridge carry more than it can.

Don't pile too much on today. Let past problems stay there, and don't worry about the future until it comes. That is a prescription for peace.

❏ **Number Two: Be willing to take unpopular stands.**

This doesn't look like peace, initially, but it's what true peacemakers do. They pull the root of the weed out; they don't just snip the top off. They go for the cure, not just a mask for the symptoms. They stand against opposition rather than caving in.

One of the college students at our church wrote a thesis on the perils of abortion, but it wasn't popular with her professor. She received a low grade, and went to the dean and showed him the paper. The dean said it was brilliant, and he overrode the professor's decision. His decision brought true peace.

One night after a Sunday service, I was walking around the sanctuary greeting people, when a man came up to me and said he didn't like a reference I made to homosexuality in the sermon. "You're stereotyping the gay community," he said.

I'm usually not riled up by those kinds of remarks, but this time something rose up in me and I decided I wasn't going to back down. I called him by name and said, "There is a Heaven and there is a hell. The Bible says that your sin is damnable. You will never go to Heaven unless you repent and turn to Jesus Christ. He'll set you free. Unless you make that decision, don't talk to me anymore about it." He was taken aback because he wasn't expecting to hear the truth. He thought I would keep the peace by not disagreeing with him.

The next altar call I gave, that man was up there crying and weeping, repenting, and turning his life over to Christ.

Sometimes peacemaking requires radical surgery to get a cure rather than just masking the symptoms. Jesus was a peacemaker, and He knew when to stand His ground and when to retreat. We should do the same.

Peace means promoting others above ourselves.

Chapter Fourteen

Blessed Are Those Who Follow The Prince Of Peace

❑ **Number Three: Be an example of forgiveness.** King Hussein of Jordan worked hard for peace before his death in the late 1990s. One time a group of young men got caught up in a radical group and threatened to kill one of the king's family members. One of the would-be assassins was caught and thrown in prison for the rest of his life. He was only eighteen or nineteen years old.

After eight months in prison, a helicopter landed in the prison yard. Guards went down to his cell and escorted him to the helicopter. The young man thought he was going to be executed. The man in the helicopter looked at him, and it was King Hussein. The pilot started flying, and the king said to the young man, "Where did you live before you did this?" The young man told him, all the while fearing that he was going to be shoved out of the helicopter. The king whispered something to the pilot, and the helicopter changed directions. The king looked at the young man and said, "What you did was terribly wrong. Nobody likes to have their family threatened, but I know you're young, you got involved with some radical groups, and I know that you would never do anything like that again." The helicopter landed in the man's neighborhood where he used to live, and the king let him go.

Later, King Hussein gave a news conference and said, "If we ever want peace in the Middle East, we Arabs have to learn something. We're always holding a grudge and seeking revenge, but if we would practice forgiveness we would have peace in the Middle East."

How many times has a fight started in your house because you held a grudge? Forgiveness is a powerful step toward peace. It dissolves any argument you have against someone.

❏ Number Four: Promote others.

On the East Coast people will go down to the beach and catch Atlantic blue crabs. The experienced crabber takes a basket, and if he catches one crab, he puts it in the basket and places a lid over it so the crab can't get out. But as soon as there's a second crab and a third crab in the basket, he doesn't bother putting the lid on anymore because whenever a crab tries to crawl out of the basket, another crab grabs it and pulls it back in! If those crabs would only learn to promote each other, they wouldn't end up on somebody's dinner table. They lack any sort of wisdom.

It would be nice to think we are smarter than crabs, but that isn't always true. Peace means promoting others above ourselves. It means making a co-worker look good at a meeting. Making sacrifices so your spouse can excel in his or her field of endeavor. You don't have to lie down and let people walk over you, but if you make their success your concern the blessings will boomerang back to you.

☐ **Number Five: Introduce people to the Prince of peace.**

In some countries when a baby girl is born it is a cause for mourning. Girls are sometimes considered less valuable than cattle because they bring no wealth to a family. So in India and other countries, there is a market for young girls to be taken to cities and turned into prostitutes. Dealers visit small villages and offer families $100 or so for their young girl, perhaps promising that they will get them good jobs. The families believe it is a sign of blessing from one of their gods, so they take the money and give away the daughter.

The girl is taken away to a big city and put into child prostitution. Businessmen from around the world will fly to these cities to have sex with very young girls, and the girls are often beaten and almost always catch AIDS and other diseases. They know nothing about peace. When they die, their bodies are literally thrown into the streets, and nobody will touch them for fear of AIDS.

When some missionaries found out about the sex trade they started buying these girls back from their owners, cleaning them up, treating them medically and teaching them about Jesus. When they were old enough, they trained them to be nurses and teachers.

One little girl was dying with AIDS and missionary David Grant went to see her before he came to the U.S. to raise support. He said, "Honey, I've got to go to America to raise more money so that we can get more people redeemed from this terrible life." She said, "I am so glad that you introduced me to Jesus. I have so much peace, but I'll never see you again. By the time you get back I'll be dead of AIDS."

Grant could only cry. He got on the plane from Calcutta, flew to New York and made his rounds. Eight months later he went back, and there was that little girl. Her weight had come back, her eyes were bright, and she ran into his arms and said, "Jesus healed me!"

That's being a peace hero. There is no better way to succeed at this lesson than by rescuing people from hopeless situations.

You and I can be heroes whether we go overseas or stay where we are. Being a hero means:

• Calming people down at work before fights occur.

• Responding to ugly talk or angry words with quiet, uplifting responses.

• Telling the people we work with and our neighbors about Jesus so that they can know peace.

• Promoting our friends and co-workers whenever we can.

• Forgiving people quickly and thoroughly.

• Taking unpopular stands when a solution is needed.

• Cultivating an atmosphere of peace in our own hearts by staying close to Jesus.

You may never save an airplane full of people from certain death, but you can be an everyday hero!

Up to this point, all of the lessons have been positive and uplifting, but next we have to look at the one I have dreaded most.

Chapter Fifteen

Blessed Are The Persecuted

Three Christian men were shoved into the bare room and told to remove their clothes from the waist up. They obeyed and the government officers then began to beat them with blow after blow until they were totally covered with blood and had gaping wounds and injuries all over their bodies.

The officers conferred and decided that the beating was not enough, so they ordered the men to be hung by their hands from the ceiling and began to hit them with rods on their backs. On and on it went until the three men were unconscious and barely breathing. Then the officers left the room, and the men were left to recover...if they could.

This ugly scene is not only factual, it has happened to Christians within the last decade. It may seem terrible to us in America, but Jesus said:

> Blessed *are* they which are persecuted for righteousness' sake: for theirs is the kingdom of heaven.
>
> Blessed are ye, when *men* shall revile you, and persecute *you*, and shall say all manner of evil against you falsely, for my sake.
>
> Rejoice, and be exceeding glad: for great *is* your reward in heaven: for so persecuted they the prophets which were before you.
>
> —Matthew 5:10-12

If there's one thing I have learned, it is that the Christian life is full of paradoxes that can't be understood by the human mind. Right after Jesus said blessed are the peacemakers, He said:

> Blessed *are* they which are persecuted...
>
> —Matthew 5:10a

Persecution comes in different forms. It doesn't always mean being tortured or killed. I remember picking up the local newspaper one time, and there was my picture on the front page. My mouth was open, I was holding my Bible up in the air, and the caption said I was a "gee-whiz, Bible-thumping entertainer." I felt the sting of being ridiculed in public, but I should have expected it. Jesus said it would happen.

Somebody told me, "Criticism is like a monster, and the only thing that can cause that monster to grow is by beating on it." One time Rex Humbard knelt down on the floor of my office and said, "Dave, I'm going to pray that God will give you a heart to forgive all the people who criticize you, because whenever you're doing something right people will speak against you."

Compared to the three men who were beaten because of their faith, my struggles and yours may seem minor; but all of us will face persecution of some kind.

The Three Promises Of Persecution

Jesus promised His followers three things.

First, He said we will be persecuted. Persecution means to pursue with hostile or abusive intent. It can range from negative body language all the way to physical execution.

I remember a man in my church who didn't like me from the moment I came on staff. He was on vacation when I became Senior Pastor, and his first words when he heard were, "Oh, no."

He tried to intimidate me during my struggling sermons as a young preacher. I'd be in the pulpit preaching my heart out, and suddenly I'd realize that I had offended him. I could tell because he would jerk his head to one side and hold it there the rest of the service.

One day I was visiting a friend in the hospital, and this man who didn't like me came down the hall. I asked what he was doing there and he said he had a kink in his neck! I don't know if God was paying him back for what he did to me, but I sure didn't see him jerking his head to the side during my sermons any more.

Many other people face much worse persecution. I read about a 22-year-old Chinese Christian evangelist who was arrested at a prayer meeting and beaten severely. The security officers then handed their clubs to the congregants and ordered them to beat him or else they would be beaten. The young evangelist was so badly injured that the security team feared he would die in their presence, so they released him. He crawled and hobbled for several miles, attempting to reach his home, but he finally collapsed and died on the road. This took place in 1994.

It is wretched and horrible, but it is a fact of the Christian life.

Reviled And Defamed

Second, Jesus said you're going to be reviled, or verbally abused and ridiculed.

I remember a man who worked at the power company with me years ago. He always had something sarcastic to say — a rib, a barb, an ill-timed word. I prayed for the man and later became pastor of Mount Hope Church, and one year during an evangelistic campaign I looked out at the people who had responded to the altar call, and there he was with tears streaming down his face. God can change revilers, those who verbally abuse you.

Third, you will face defamation. I used to think that if you did everything right, people would speak well of you. Then I read Luke 6:26a, where Jesus said, "Woe unto you, when all men shall speak well of you!" If you are doing everything right, you're going to be lied about and defamed! They will lie about your motives, try to cheapen your generosity, plant doubts about you and try to sully your name. Expect it!

How many of us think success is winning friends and influencing people? Jesus turned that on its head and said success is winning enemies!

Why They Do It

Why do persecutors persecute, revilers revile and defamers defame? Because your godly life provokes them. David said:

> Every day they wrest my words: all their thoughts *are* against me for evil.
>
> —Psalm 56:5

There may be no cause, but there is a reason, and that reason is they are convicted, shamed and angered by your righteousness. Cain killed his brother, Abel, because Abel was righteous (I John 3:12). It is less work for someone to criticize you than to change his own life.

Strangely enough, much of the persecution Christians face comes from within the church. I frequently get letters from people wanting to know why there isn't a cross hanging in the sanctuary of my church. They want to know if I have a problem with the cross; if I'm ashamed of it. Absolutely not! We put a cross on the video screen when we're singing, and there are crosses all over our building, but there's not a permanent cross in the main sanctuary.

The cross is a symbol of Roman execution, but the cross didn't die for our sins — Jesus did. I doubt that the early church had crosses hung in their meeting places. People who make the symbol of the cross more important than the Man who hung on it are getting their order wrong. And yet I field criticism for not having a cross on the wall of our sanctuary.

Christians persecute each other because of jealousy. Joseph's brothers sold him into slavery because they were jealous. Jealousy motivated Cain's murder. I often observe that people come to our church in financial difficulty, accept Christ, get filled with the Holy Spirit, and start learning God's economic principles. When they get back on their feet financially, they are persecuted by their old friends and family members who want them to stay in poverty. That reminds me of the crabs in the bucket, pulling each other down!

There are numerous other reasons people will persecute you. Maybe they are rebelling against God. Maybe they are losing business because of the Church, like the silversmiths who made miniature idols in Paul's day. When the Gospel gripped that city, they realized nobody would buy their idols, so they ran Paul out of town.

Whatever the reason, we should rejoice when we are persecuted. God guarantees character development during times of verbal abuse, criticism, attack, and defamation. In the next chapter, we'll talk about how to handle persecution.

Chapter Sixteen

Blessed Are Those Who Handle Persecution Properly

Every movie has a bad guy who spends most of the story making things miserable for the good guy. The moment we all wait for is when the bad guy finally gets his due. There's nothing better than seeing him squirm after all the unfair stuff he's done.

But some movies are more complex. The villain is a little more sympathetic, and we don't exactly want him to suffer, even though we know he should. The climax of those films is when the bad guy has a change of heart and becomes a good guy. We feel his redemption and have an abundance of good will toward him.

That's what happens to persecutors. They either get saved or they get their due.

Saul of Tarsus was a persecutor who got saved and became Saint Paul. James, the brother of Jesus, was a persecutor early on — he said Jesus was insane — but when He died and rose from the dead, James became a believer and a pillar in the church.

A man I once knew hated to hear people talk about God. One day I mentioned something church-related, and he got angry. The veins in his neck stuck out, and he said he was tired of hearing about religion, about church, about Jesus. I backed off and let God work on him, and today the man is an usher in the church and a good friend of mine.

But there are the other persecutors who don't repent. Jezebel persecuted Elijah because he slaughtered her false prophets. She had opportunities to repent but she didn't, and she died a gruesome death, with dogs licking her blood off of the ground.

A group of rebels persecuted Moses, and the earth opened up and swallowed them and their families. They missed their chance to repent.

God takes pleasure in persecuting those who persecute us. The Bible says the angel of the Lord is going to persecute the persecutor (Psalm 35:3-6).

> **Seeing *it is* a righteous thing with God to recompense tribulation to them that trouble you...**
>
> **—II Thessalonians 1:6**

The Psalms say His arrows will fly against the persecutor (7:13), and they will perish at the presence of God (9:1-3). Worst of all, they will stand at the great white throne of judgment before God, where sinners are banished to hell forever (Revelation 20:11-15).

When you remember that, you start to have sympathy for even your worst critics.

What To Do

How do we handle persecution? To be honest, my stomach goes into knots, and I get angry. I want to lash back, vindicate myself and call down curses on my persecutors.

Then I remember — Jesus said this would happen. Why do I act like it's unusual? The first key to handling persecution is this: Expect it.

Polycarp was a Christian pastor in Smyrna during the time of the Roman Empire, and he was dragged before the Roman magistrate and told to make an offering unto Caesar or face the penalty. He said, "Eighty-six years I have served the Lord Jesus Christ and He has never done me wrong. How could I blaspheme my Lord by offering a sacrifice to man?" So they sentenced him to burn at the stake. One of his young assistants knew that Polycarp was going to be burned and said, "If God's grace is truly sufficient, lift up one finger so I'll know when I face it that God's grace will be sufficient for me."

They tied Polycarp to the stake, put the wood around his feet, built up the kindling and lit it on fire. Polycarp stood in the midst of the flame, smiling as if he didn't feel anything. He looked over at his assistant and he held up three fingers, meaning God's grace is not only sufficient; it's more than enough.

You can expect to be persecuted. You're probably not going to be killed, but it's possible that you might.

First, remember that all persecution is temporary.

> For our light affliction, which is but for a moment, worketh for us a far more exceeding *and* eternal weight of glory.
>
> —II Corinthians 4:17

Persecution may seem like it never ends, but it's just for a season. When it's over, the reward will far outweigh the pain.

Second, (this is the important one!), rejoice and be exceedingly glad.

James put it this way:

> My brethren, count it all joy when ye fall into divers temptations.
>
> —James 1:2

When someone verbally abuses you, go back to your office and shout for joy. When they bad-mouth your church, go in your backyard and leap around. Why?

• *Because a miracle is in the works.* Paul and Silas were beaten and put in jail. Did they complain that God let them fall into the mess? No, they sang praises, rejoicing, being glad that they were counted worthy to suffer for Jesus Christ. Little did they know that as they rejoiced, a miracle was stirring. An earthquake broke off their shackles, swung the jail door open and caused a revival in the jailer's family!

• *Because God is enlarging your influence, ministry and character.* David said:

> ...thou hast enlarged me when I was in distress...
>
> —Psalm 4:1b

There's no way to grow quite like when you're being persecuted. When I went through an extremely difficult time early in my pastoring career, I felt so isolated and wounded that I finally went into a Sunday school room, threw myself on the floor and asked God why there was such intense persecution. The voice of the Lord came to me and said, "You have endured it, and I have doubled your anointing."

I didn't feel like my anointing had doubled, and I wondered later if it was my own imagination. But the next Sunday I walked into the pulpit, and there were more people in church than I'd ever seen. I gave the invitation to accept Christ, and twice as many people responded as had ever responded before. That started a period of phenomenal growth in our church.

This lesson may seem like the most uninviting one, but it's the one from which we receive the fullest blessings. No pain is welcome at the time, but Jesus tells us that it is well worth it. When you are persecuted, be happy! You are following in the footsteps of Jesus.

The Last Word

Here we are on the last day before finals. All the lessons of Success 101 have been taught. All the research has been done. What's left?

One last thing. *It's time to take action!*

There was a woman who had been born with a physical defect that caused blindness, but as technology advanced, doctors found a way to reverse it. She decided to have the surgery and made an appointment with the doctor. When he was finished, she sat on the edge of her hospital bed and let him take the bandages off her eyes. For the first time, she saw light, color, faces, smiles. It was as though her life had just begun.

The tragedy of the story is this: The procedure for reversing her blindness had been available for twenty years. She could have regained her sight when she was thirty, but she waited until she was fifty.

Don't be like her. You have the keys to being successful. Use them now! Here's a quick review:

- Be teachable and trusting.

- Admit your personal inadequacy.

- Go through times of mourning with the right balance.

- Sow seeds of faith in times of sorrow.

- Give other people a break.

- Be gentle, unassuming and unobtrusive.

- Be sensitive toward God and His authority.

- Develop a hearty spiritual appetite.

- Show mercy to those who don't deserve it.

- Put yourself in the path of purity.

- Be a peace hero.

- Take unpopular stands for your beliefs.

- Promote others when you can.

- Be very happy when you are persecuted, reviled, and defamed.

These, Jesus said, are the keys to happiness. You have now graduated with a diploma in Success 101. May God's richest rewards be yours as you put these lessons into practice!

About The Author

Dave Williams is pastor of Mount Hope Church and International Outreach Ministries, with world headquarters in Lansing, Michigan. He has served for over 20 years, leading the church in Lansing from 226 to over 4000 today. Dave sends trained ministers into unreached cities to establish disciple-making churches, and, as a result, today has "branch" churches in the United States, Philippines, and in Africa.

Dave is the founder and president of Mount Hope Bible Training Institute, a fully accredited institute for training ministers and lay people for the work of the ministry. He has authored 55 books including the fifteen-time best seller, *The New Life...The Start of Something Wonderful* (with over 2,000,000 books sold), and more recently, *The Miracle Results of Fasting, The Road To Radical Riches,* and *Angels*.

The Pacesetter's Path telecast is Dave's weekly television program seen over a syndicated network of secular stations, and nationally over the Sky Angel satellite system. Dave has produced over 125 audio cassette programs including the nationally acclaimed *School of Pacesetting Leadership* which is being used as a training program in churches around the United States, and in Bible Schools in South Africa and the Philippines. He is a popular speaker at conferences, seminars, and conventions. His speaking ministry has taken him across America, Africa, Europe, Asia, and other parts of the world.

Along with his wife, Mary Jo, Dave established The Dave and Mary Jo Williams Charitable Mission (Strategic Global Mission), a mission's ministry for providing scholarships to pioneer pastors and grants to inner-city children's ministries.

Dave's articles and reviews have appeared in national magazines such as *Advance, The Pentecostal Evangel, Ministries Today, The Lansing Magazine, The Detroit Free Press* and others. Dave, as a private pilot, flies for fun. He is married, has two grown children, and lives in Delta Township, Michigan.

You may write to Pastor Dave Williams:

P.O. Box 80825

Lansing, MI 48908-0825

Please include your special prayer requests when you write, or you may call the Mount Hope Global Prayer Center: (517) 327-PRAY

For Your Spiritual Growth

Here's the help you need for your spiritual journey. These books will encourage you, and give you guidance as you seek to draw close to Jesus and learn of Him. Prepare yourself for fantastic growth!

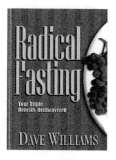

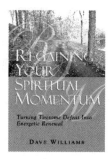

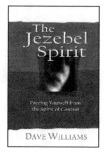

RADICAL FASTING
How would you like to achieve your dreams at "break-neck" speed? Radical fasting may be your key!

REGAINING YOUR SPIRITUAL MOMENTUM
Use this remarkable book as your personal street map to regain your spiritual momentum.

THE JEZEBEL SPIRIT
Do you feel controlled? Learn more about what the Bible says about this manipulating principality's influence.

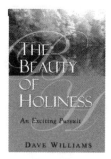

DEVELOPING THE SPIRIT OF A CONQUEROR
Take back what the enemy has stolen from you. Learn how to engage your authority and *Develop the Spirit of a Conqueror*.

BEAUTY OF HOLINESS
We face the choice — holiness or rebellion. True holiness comes about by working together in cooperation with the Holy Spirit.

ABCs OF SUCCESS & HAPPINESS
God wants to give you every good gift, so it's time to accept the responsibility for your success today!

For Your Spiritual Growth

Here's the help you need for your spiritual journey. These books will encourage you, and give you guidance as you seek to draw close to Jesus and learn of Him. Prepare yourself for fantastic growth!

QUESTIONS I HAVE ANSWERED
Get answers to many of the questions you've always wanted to ask a pastor!

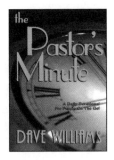

THE PASTOR'S MINUTE
A daily devotional for people on the go! Powerful topics will help you grow even when you're in a hurry.

ANGELS: THEY ARE WATCHING YOU!
The Bible tells more than you might think about these powerful beings.

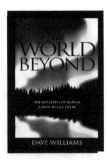

THE WORLD BEYOND
What will Heaven be like? What happens there? Will we see relatives who have gone before us? Who *REALLY* goes to Heaven?

FILLED!
Learn how you can be filled with the mightiest power in the universe. Find out what could be missing from your life.

STRATEGIC GLOBAL MISSION
Read touching stories about God's plan for accelerating the Gospel globally through reaching children and training pastors.

These and other books available from Dave Williams and:

DECAPOLIS PUBLISHING

For Your Spiritual Growth

Here's the help you need for your spiritual journey. These books will encourage you, and give you guidance as you seek to draw close to Jesus and learn of Him. Prepare yourself for fantastic growth!

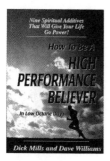

HOW TO BE A HIGH PERFORMANCE BELIEVER
Pour in the nine spiritual additives for real power in your Christian life.

SECRET OF POWER WITH GOD
Tap into the real power with God; the power of prayer. It will change your life!

THE NEW LIFE...
You can get off to a great start on your exciting life with Jesus! Prepare for something wonderful.

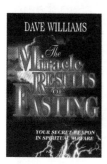

MIRACLE RESULTS OF FASTING
You can receive MIRACLE benefits, spiritually and physically, with this practical Christian discipline.

WHAT TO DO IF YOU MISS THE RAPTURE
If you miss the Rapture, there may still be hope, but you need to follow these clear survival tactics.

THE AIDS PLAGUE
Is there hope? Yes, but only Jesus can bring a total and lasting cure to AIDS.

These and other books available from Dave Williams and:

DECAPOLIS PUBLISHING

For Your Spiritual Growth

Here's the help you need for your spiritual journey. These books will encourage you, and give you guidance as you seek to draw close to Jesus and learn of Him. Prepare yourself for fantastic growth!

THE ART OF PACESETTING LEADERSHIP
You can become a successful leader with this proven leadership development course.

GIFTS THAT SHAPE YOUR LIFE
Learn which ministry best fits you, and discover your God-given personality gifts, as well as the gifts of others.

GROWING UP IN OUR FATHER'S FAMILY
You can have a family relationship with your heavenly father. Learn how God cares for you.

SUPERNATURAL SOULWINNING
How will we reach our family, friends, and neighbors in this short time before Christ's return?

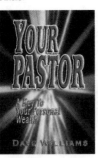

YOUR PASTOR: A KEY TO YOUR PERSONAL WEALTH
By honoring your pastor you can actually be setting yourself up for a financial blessing from God!

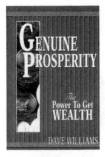

GENUINE PROSPERITY
Learn what it means to be truly prosperous! God gives us the power to get wealth!

These and other books available from Dave Williams and:

DECAPOLIS PUBLISHING

For Your Spiritual Growth

Here's the help you need for your spiritual journey. These books will encourage you, and give you guidance as you seek to draw close to Jesus and learn of Him. Prepare yourself for fantastic growth!

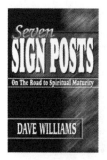

SOMEBODY OUT THERE NEEDS YOU
Along with the gift of salvation comes the great privilege of spreading the gospel of Jesus Christ.

SEVEN SIGNPOSTS TO SPIRITUAL MATURITY
Examine your life to see where you are on the road to spiritual maturity.

THE PASTORS PAY
How much is your pastor worth? Who should set his pay? Discover the scriptural guidelines for paying your pastor.

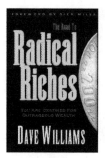

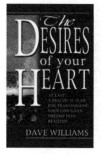

DECEPTION, DELUSION & DESTRUCTION
Recognize spiritual deception and unmask spiritual blindness.

THE ROAD TO RADICAL RICHES
Are you ready to jump from "barely getting by" to Gods plan for putting you on the road to Radical Riches?

THE DESIRES OF YOUR HEART
Yes, Jesus wants to give you the desires of your heart, and make them realities.

These and other books available from Dave Williams and:

DECAPOLIS PUBLISHING

For Your Successful Life

These video cassettes will give you successful principles to apply to your whole life. Each a different topic, and each a fantastic teaching of how living by God's Word can give you total success!

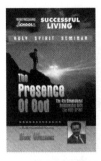

THE PRESENCE OF GOD
Find out how you can have a more dynamic relationship with the Holy Spirit.

FILLED WITH THE HOLY SPIRIT
You can rejoice and share with others in this wonderful experience of God.

GIFTS THAT CHANGE YOUR WORLD
Learn which ministry best fits you, and discover your God-given personality gifts, as well as the gifts of others.

THE SCHOOL OF PACESETTING LEADERSHIP
Leaders are made, not born. You can become a successful leader with this proven leadership development course.

MIRACLE RESULTS OF FASTING
Fasting is your secret weapon in spiritual warfare. Learn how you'll benefit spiritually and physically! Six video messages.

A SPECIAL LADY
If you feel used and abused, this video will show you how you really are in the eyes of Jesus. You are special!

These and other videos available from Dave Williams and:

DECAPOLIS
PUBLISHING

For Your Successful Life

These video cassettes will give you successful principles to apply to your whole life. Each a different topic, and each a fantastic teaching of how living by God's Word can give you total success!

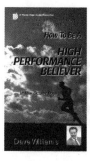

HOW TO BE A HIGH PERFORMANCE BELIEVER
Pour in the nine spiritual additives for real power in your Christian life.

THE UGLY WORMS OF JUDGMENT
Recognizing the decay of judgment in your life is your first step back into God's fullness.

WHAT TO DO WHEN YOU FEEL WEAK AND DEFEATED
Learn about God's plan to bring you out of defeat and into His principles of victory!

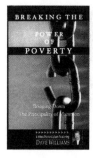

WHY SOME ARE NOT HEALED
Discover the obstacles that hold people back from receiving their miracle and how God can help them receive the very best!

BREAKING THE POWER OF POVERTY
The principality of mammon will try to keep you in poverty. Put God FIRST and watch Him bring you into a wealthy place.

HERBS FOR HEALTH
A look at the concerns and fears of modern medicine. Learn the correct ways to open the doors to your healing.

These and other videos available from Dave Williams and:

DECAPOLIS PUBLISHING

Running Your Race

These simple but powerful audio cassette singles will help give you the edge you need. Run your race to win!

LONELY IN THE MIDST OF A CROWD
Loneliness is a devastating disease. Learn how to trust and count on others to help.

HERBS FOR HEALTH
A look at the concerns and fears of modern medicine. Learn the correct ways to open the doors to your healing.

HOW TO GET ANYTHING YOU WANT
You can learn the way to get anything you want from God!

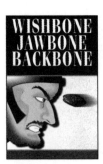

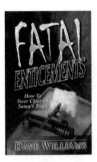

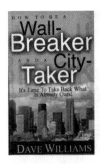

WISHBONE, JAWBONE, BACKBONE
Learn about King David, and how his three "bones" for success can help you in your life quest.

FATAL ENTICEMENTS
Learn how you can avoid the vice-like grip of sin and it's fatal enticements that hold people captive.

HOW TO BE A WALL BREAKER AND A CITY TAKER
You can be a powerful force for advancing the Kingdom of Jesus Christ!

These and other audio tapes available from Dave Williams and:

DECAPOLIS
PUBLISHING

Expanding Your Faith

These exciting audio teaching series will help you to grow and mature in your walk with Christ. Get ready for amazing new adventures in faith!

THE BLESSING
Explore the many ways that God can use you to bless others, and how He can correct the missed blessing.

SIN'S GRIP
Learn how you can avoid the vice-like grip of sin and it's fatal enticements that hold people captive.

FAITH, HOPE, & LOVE
Listen and let these three "most important things in life" change you.

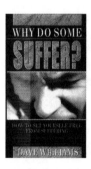

**PSALM 91
THE PROMISE OF
PROTECTION**
Everyone is looking for protection in these perilous times. God promises protection for those who rest in Him.

**DEVELOPING
THE SPIRIT OF A
CONQUEROR**
You can be a conqueror through Christ! Also, find out how to *keep* those things that you have conquered.

WHY DO SOME SUFFER
Find out why some people seem to have suffering in their lives, and find out how to avoid it in your life.

These and other audio tapes available from Dave Williams and:

DECAPOLIS
PUBLISHING

Expanding Your Faith

These exciting audio teaching series will help you to grow and mature in your walk with Christ. Get ready for amazing new adventures in faith!

ABCs OF SUCCESS AND HAPPINESS
Learn how to go after God's promises for your life. Happiness and success can be yours today!

FORGIVENESS
The miracle remedy for many of life's problems is found in this basic key for living.

UNTANGLING YOUR TROUBLES
You can be a "trouble untangler" with the help of Jesus!

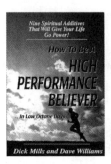

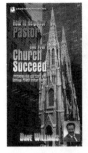

HOW TO BE A HIGH PERFORMANCE BELIEVER
Put in the nine spiritual additives to help run your race and get the prize!

BEING A DISCIPLE AND MAKING DISCIPLES
You can learn to be a "disciple maker" to almost anyone.

HOW TO HELP YOUR PASTOR & CHURCH SUCCEED
You can be an integral part of your church's & pastor's success.

These and other audio tapes available from Dave Williams and:

DECAPOLIS PUBLISHING